Looking for Home
Journey and Boundary in Postmodern Texts

Edited by
Siddhartha Biswas

ATLANTIC
PUBLISHERS & DISTRIBUTORS (P) LTD

Published by
ATLANTIC
PUBLISHERS & DISTRIBUTORS (P) LTD
7/22, Ansari Road, Darya Ganj, New Delhi-110002
Phones : +91-11-40775252, 40775214, 23273880, 23275880
Fax : +91-11-23285873
Web : www.atlanticbooks.com
E-mail : orders@atlanticbooks.com

Branch Office: Chennai
Phones : +91-44-48531784, 28291383
E-mail : chennai@atlanticbooks.com

Printed & bound in India by Atlantic Print Services

Dedicated to
Trailakya Mohan Biswas and
Sima Biswas, and all those who
struggled to create a Home

Acknowledgements

I must begin by expressing my gratitude to all the contributors. The term 'contributor' in no way does justice to the relationship I share with each and every one of them. I am indeed fortunate that I can call all of them my friends. Irrespective of their temporal locations as well as temperamental situations, they all agreed to be a part of this project and tolerated my often inconvenient demands. The articles that find a place in this book are insightful, critical, and academically relevant. They offer not only a look at literature, but also at life. I would also like to thank those who could not, for some reason or the other, finally present their articles. All of them invested serious thoughts and encouraged me to move forward. Despite harrowing schedules, the fact that they considered contributing to this volume is appreciable. I have had valuable discussions with many of my colleagues and my peers regarding the concept that is the core of this book. I owe them a large debt of gratitude.

My friends at Atlantic have also extended remarkable support. Their professionalism, not devoid of affability, has been extremely impressive. Without them this book would not have seen the light of day. I offer them my sincerest thanks.

Siddhartha Biswas

Contents

Acknowledgements .... *iv*

Introduction .... *vii*

List of Contributors .... *xvi*

Exclusion and Migration: The De-Constructed Home

1. "What have we to do with Pakistan? We were born here": Exodus Revisited in Khushwant Singh's *Train to Pakistan* 3
   Paramita Dutta
2. Making a Journey and Resisting It: Ambiguity and Paradox in Kazuo Ishiguro's *A Pale View of Hills*..... 15
   Sharanya Dutta
3. From Bangladesh to Brick Lane: Leaving the Home in Search of a New World 24
   Trayee Sinha
4. Ashima and Alienation in Jhumpa Lahiri's *The Namesake*: From Myth to Modernity 34
   Mohona Chatterjee

Being at Home: (Dis)Locating the Self

5. Exile is Not Home: A Reading of Chinua Achebe's *Home and Exile* 47
   Debaditya Mukhopadhyay
6. Displacement and Madness: Situating (Mad) Woman Outside the Attic.. 56
   Samata Biswas

7. The Eternal Quest: Home and the Homeless in Amitav Ghosh's *The Hungry Tide* 64
Zenith Roy

8. Run Forrest Run: To Home and Away 75
Susmita Paul

9. Life's Tentative Journeys: The Fable-Fact Interface in Paulo Coelho's *The Alchemist* 86
Rudrashis Datta

10. The Ones Who Fell Through: Home of the Dispossessed in Arundhati Roy's *The Ministry of Utmost Happiness* 94
Arpa Ghosh

11. Home and Identity in Ritwik Ghatak's Films 106
Pritha Kundu

12. Undesirable Aliens: Fissures of Nation, Polis and Self in *District 9* 118
Abin Chakraborty

Reinventing Location: Texts in Search of a Home

13. From *Heart of Darkness* to *Apocalypse Now*: The Changing Face of Text-ness 133
Sagnik Banerjee

14. Comics Journalism and the Question of Authenticity: A Reading of Joe Sacco's *Safe Area Goražde* 150
Saikat Sarkar

15. Anxiety of Acceptance: Recent Popular Representations of Gothic on Screen 168
Nivedita Bachhar

16. Outward Journey Inward: Blurred Boundaries in Italo Calvino's *If on a Winter's Night a Traveller* 175
Rishiraj Pal

17. Shifting Locations—Cordelia from *King Lear* to *Lear* 184
Siddhartha Biswas

Introduction

Home and location have been indispensable elements in all art of all ages, particularly in literature. The early migration stories and the political movements from one point to various others as found in the epics slowly evolved into the quest themes of the middle ages. Trade expeditions laced with missionary and colonial intentions became frantic during the fifteenth and sixteenth centuries—as did the corresponding literature that justified the actions to the individual as well as national consciences. But narratives regarding travel—and not travelogues, which have their own dynamic—took on a whole new dimension in the postmodern era. The journey motif itself has myriad connotations and, whether it is inbound or outbound, it always carries the primary question of purpose. The traveller may have a variety of reasons to travel. Travelling for temporary escape is one thing—something that has been elegantly formulated by William Wordsworth—but travelling as exile is quite different. The entire dynamic is now drastically changed because the structure that was automatically assumed in earlier times, with a defined return to a securely defined home, is non-existent for a number of the present migrant-travellers. Also, travelling towards a destination with a definite goal in mind always brings in the question of whether the traveller is willingly inclined to travel or not. Migration is always necessity-oriented, and such journeys presuppose one goal—that of finding or re-establishing home. In this process, there are quite a few issues, including postcolonial ones that foreground themselves. The complication finds extension in the idea of trans-nationalism, in the fact that there is now present a generation of people who are comfortable surviving in multiple identities—hyphenated identities as it is often called. Their location in the socio-historical process is still under scrutiny. They promise to play a pivotal role in the days to come.

Among these one may posit the following issue first—whether the migrant is excluded and forced to look for a new home or is it a conscious and deliberated escape on the migrant's part. The reasons can be manifold—political, emotional, economic, academic, and so on. The choice to leave is ruled by greed or hope for sanctuary in the face of a variety of persecution. Secondly, the adopted home often becomes inadequate and one must journey back or onward to find one's true identity. With locational distancing the self often becomes dysfunctional, whereas in certain cases similar journeys become fundamental in finding the self. In fact, the idea of home and homeland shifts with time, and often we see new boundaries are created (or re-visioned) to accommodate ethno-religious politics which results in forced migrations and widespread trauma. The pain, the wonder, the suffering, the bewilderment, the ghetto-creation, and the continuous reinvention of the self within and outside homelands, irrespective of geopolitical locationing, are all part of the baggage of a postmodern traveller.

Cultural differences and deflections, hybridization, victimization, and construction of the other in terms of whole new margin-formations are all seen extensively explored in the literature of today. History often functions as the other location. Going back to the past texts to comprehend the present is not new, but it is a significant part in the process of home-making. And such movements are instrumental in much of the new literature. This brings us to the third major issue. One of the most crucial movements lies in the case of the texts and the literary figures contained within them which now travel from their established positions and find themselves reinvented in form and management—and this process is not an inconsequential journey in the life of contemporary humanity. This exploration, looking for location in the earlier texts, has its own political agenda and sheds much light on the whole migration question—for relocation of texts is one of the key migrations that we see now. And they are undertaken not in the fashion of earlier days. Now, the texts travel stripped of their initial identity, much like their human counterparts. They are adopted, adapted, recreated, and transcreated; and in these processes we have a whole new quest for identity-formation. The migration of food, literature, and all such intellectual expressions speak of a cultural movement that is a result of political negotiations—conscious and subconscious. The making of a home is not independent of such tropes and in such movements one can find the foundation of the home-idea. The new homes, and the strain/appeal of the old ones, and the pull of the path that takes us both ways, are the very issues that dictate much of the life of the planet. This is so because, quite unfortunately, home can no longer be as easily constructed or securely maintained; and that demands exploration.

When Amish wrote the *Shiva Trilogy*, he, probably without realizing its full consequence, was entering the world of a very postmodern political scenario—that of redefinition. He was rationalizing and re-mythifying an established, in fact, institutionalized religion. The agenda was to bring the myth closer to the contemporary world; to relocate a legend turned myth turned holy into something familiar, tangible, without violating its holiness. And in a country as sensitive as India, where things become unclean by the mere touch of the taboo, and where that violation can easily translate into legitimized violence, the lack of noise regarding such reinvention is in itself a pointer to its political success and the agenda that lurks behind.

Such reinvention is a common postmodern and post-postmodern trope. If one was to analyze why such reinvention is required one would stumble over quite a few interesting aspects. In fact, in a world where the hunger for the new is so vicious that creators cannot cope rationally and adequately, the old has become a goldmine of material. Beginning from rehashes, remixes, remakes, and reboots we come to the disparate and sometimes jarring inventions. Popular culture is the biggest playing field of such activities. But, even in other areas one sees challenges to different conservative and established notions. Literature, rather the Arts are now looking at new possibilities, breaking away from traditional boundaries. Cinema is entering the world of poetry and theatre. Photography is delving into styles of painting. Core literature is seeing free mingling of forms along with thematic explorations. The old, conventional, and set patterns are all changing. Determining, confirming, and instituting identities are the most necessary requirements of the day as the older establishments now find deep-rooted corruption and manipulation, apart from the fact that many of them should have been obsolete years back; and to add that newer notions keep challenging the structure every day. In the face of such intense changes, the question of individual identity has become a sensitive factor and much of the artistic establishment is trying to find resolution. The old is a safe option which can be re-modelled, and such re-modelling in various artistic forms is not only cheap utilization showing poverty of imagination, but also symptomatic of the need for a new construction.

But, it is not merely the hunger for the new that necessitates such reinvention. Over the last few decades the world has moved—in quite a breakneck pace—to newer agendas, particularly as far as identity and the idea of 'home' is concerned. The idea of 'home' and 'homeland' are perhaps now considered to be mutually inclusive, but the 'home' paradigm is much more internalized and therefore personal, whereas the 'homeland' paradigm is more structurally defined and now involves nation-oriented politics. The acceptance of homeland is perhaps much more intellectual and in some cases quite a compromise, whereas feeling at home is something denied to many. In a person's psychological construction, the idea of being home defines the creation of his own view of himself, the internal identity, as opposed to the naturalized or adopted citizenship that arises out of circumstances, greed or compromised. Of course, the new locations have their own set of responses and quite often that creates the dominant ghetto-creations that we see in our world today. In this world of diaspora, immigration, migration, and exclusion, the 'home' paradigm is apparently the most vital, even though it is completely intangible and unquantifiable in its intensely personal nature, as it is the only index that shows how adjusted or contented the individual is in his new, or old, surroundings. Migration is not the only issue at hand at the moment as the changing times continue to create newer spaces even within the old, and circumstances may suddenly change an amiable location into someplace directly or indirectly hostile. The journey from is as important as the journey to; for people are made homeless for very little in this world.

Much of twentieth century literature has recorded the idea of a failed adjustment on the part of the individual as well as on part of the structure. The twentieth century has seen upheavals like no other frame of time preceding it. The entire geopolitical scenario has been subjected to massive amounts of epoch-changing activity. Although history is still in the process of recording it, we still find more humane and actual portraiture in literature. And considering the contemporary politics of history, the accusation against literary perspective is beginning to look weak. The author's point of view is now something that colours history as well, and not in a personal sense but in a manner that is entirely dictated by hegemonic positions. Literature is also subject to that, but since it does not have the responsibility of being factual representation and is permitted to carry personal angst, it becomes a source that can be allowed reliability and can be, thus, analyzed. History demands, in fact commands, obedience and frowns upon those who question it—a reason why all the powers-that-be are hell bent on re-creating it to suit their purposes. This is a policy that begins with attempting to erase the memory of the holocaust that disneyfies classical mythologies and brings religious politics within the ordinary circle through television for both children and adults; and this is a policy which objects to and vilifies any work of art that does not align itself to the dictated standards.

There is the other issue of immediacy as well. Whereas migration and such movements are a continuous process which began firmly in the past, the question of relocation is fairly recent. Relocation is a fact of history, but one may argue that after the ancient migration age and the confirmation of the world order, post-Renaissance is the time when another great paradigm shift can be seen all around the globe. It is uncertain that a new paradigm would appear; it may well be that the old paradigm manages to resurface through extreme exercise of violence. The failure of communism and democracy has created a vacuum that is yet to be filled. The corporatization of global politics is a fact that can no longer be ignored. However, it is the common individual who finds him/herself in the melting pot living either in confusion, or in denial. The idea of home is very much political and politically constructed, and that is becoming a factor in much of day to day living. Understanding this anxiety is necessary. And the literature bears the best witness to this disquiet.

This anxiety is presented through reinventions and reinterpretations. However, it is difficult for any psyche forming within the subcontinental history to disregard the Partition issue. Therefore, the first segment of the book, dealing with 'Exclusion and Migration—the Deconstructed Home' begins with the event that remains a scar, even though popular memory may be slowly removing itself from the actual massacres. The Partition, which affected both the Eastern and Western fringes of the idea floated as 'nation India', has been discussed in myriad scholarly inspections hailing from both literary and socio-scientific angles. The cause and causality of the event, the euphoria and the trauma, and all such have found expression both in history and literature and they have also been seen from completely individual points of view. They represent perhaps the greatest crisis of home-construction in this part of the world and probably will find parallel only in the issues related to Judaic migration. There are a number of literary masterpieces that capture the time and the trauma, but Khushwant Singh's *Train to Pakistan* shows the horror of the 'journey' and of the final destination. The cry for not only a new home or a lost home or lives that fail to shift, but the intense sadness of that left behind, presents the crisis that has crafted the present world.

From there one can move into the core discussion that the present hypothesis demands. Ideas concerning homeland, displacement, journey, and such concepts have created a number of communities, often imagined, and the establishment of such communities has not always created home-spaces for individuals. Khushwant Singh's *The Train to Pakistan* still carries the trauma of migration and needs to be the starting point of any discussion on such events. There are a number of texts which deal with the person negotiating with the new community imagining itself to mimic the homeland. Monica Ali's *Brick Lane* and Jhumpa

Lahiri's *The Namesake* explore the individual's exploration of the new home as well as his/her own location vis-à-vis that place. *The Namesake* is a question of a new identity, a new home, and its tensions with the cultural baggage that a confirmed tradition always tries to assert over the creation of the self. Somewhat similar is the negotiation between the past and present as we see in Kazuo Ishiguro's *A Pale View of Hills*. With a genocide in the backdrop, the text moves through the experiences of multiple generations with an almost lyrical fluidity, while establishing significant queries regarding the identity of the dislocated. All three texts deal with a movement from the East to the West. These are migrations that have been the focus of much textual and political debate and they create a point of entry to the concept of home that this book is trying to interrogate.

The idea of home and exile find complete focus in Chinua Achebe's *Home and Exile*. Speaking of reverse migration, this book introduces us to the dislocation that the migrants continue to feel. The adopted home does not always become home. And the individual's quest sometimes finds the answer in elements that are inherent. Jean Rhys's *Wide Sargasso Sea* takes us through another kind of migration where the issue of identity and the issue of self find trauma within and without. There are a large number of people who are the outcome of migration and consequent associations. They have the unique problem of having no home, as they have no homeland to fall back on to. Quite often they are rejected by both cultures and must find the strength to create a space of their own. But, this process is fraught with difficulty and the result is often catastrophic. Amitav Ghosh's *The Hungry Tide* is an excellent look at the expatriate mind and the complex interrelations that such acculturation and deculturation can generate. Although it helps to include an objective point of view free of political history, yet it can lead to tragic consequences as the paradigms clash and psyches misconstrue behavior patterns.

Interestingly, the alienation aspect and the consequent 'homelessness' can occur even within the homeland and home-space. Winston Groom's *Forrest Gump* deals with this movement which generates and initiates a question of rightness. But, when the individual completely fails to conform to the new, to which he or she is not willingly attached, the result can be complete withdrawal or nostalgia laced with unreality. Of course, there are explorations which take us out of the concrete world and let us take a look at the universal constructs. The questionable pop-philosophical solace can be found in the quest for home in novels such as Paulo Coelho's *The Alchemist*. Such simplistic solutions should not be accepted without critical inquiry, more so since the popularity of such is nothing less than phenomenal. Arundhati Roy's *The Ministry of Utmost Happiness* gives us a brand new look at the idea and truth of dislocation. Ritwik Ghatak's films still continue to provide the perfect expression for the anguish that left generations searching and still remain a kind of paradigm for those who are lost and those who are trying to lose themselves into a new space. Although they are also about the partition, still the homelessness that they present remains equally applicable to the new-migrants. The much-discussed text of *District 9*—Neill Blomkamp's 2009 film—is quite obviously a work on dislocation and the ghettoization that has been such a great part of human history. Using the science-fiction format, Blomkamp literally turns the aliens into off-world aliens and creates a parable about apartheid. Here the aliens become refuge-seekers instead of colonial or marauding powers, yet the xenophobia and the hatred they generate becomes an allegory for asylum seekers everywhere.

Journey and home are concepts no longer limited to mankind. In this age of global correspondence, literature, in fact the Arts, is also travelling through a kind of unique fluidity. And we see reinventions of artistic forms, genres, tropes, styles, and such reinventions seem to be the accepted form rather than the original. The Gothic is now taking on a different avatar. With television and cinema appropriating the Gothic, what we have is a very loaded retelling of the classic stories. The point of interest is that these stories take on issues of identity and homelessness through a 'repackaging' of the established theme. The novel has given way to the graphic novel, and the cinema with its newly allotted textness is becoming and sometimes appropriating the comfort and privilege of earlier texts—as in the case of *Apocalypse Now* and *Heart of Darkness*. Africa seamlessly migrates into

Asia. The colonial gaze does not change and the texts that the dominant power creates adhere to the same strategic plots. In this context, no one can ignore Italo Calvino's *If on a Winter's Night a Traveler*. We also have textual entities travelling over time and finding themselves redefined and relocated as in the case of Lear and Cordelia in Edward Bond's *Lear*. This, of course, is an area not to be dealt with quickly, but entirely ignoring it is also unacceptable as these show us the process of contemporary construction, how the new absorbs the old, how tradition is manipulated and how social evolution is being effected at the very moment.

Life on this planet is ever-changing. However, the dynamic of new identity-formation has never been this vigorous. Whereas there is a large amount of largely economically motivated movement, there is also great political and ethnic resistance to the settlers. The conflict is no longer entirely xenophobia or race-related. Now, the negotiation is much more complex, and it is on a more personal level since the later generations of migrants are asking new questions regarding their own identity. The immediate past—and in some cases the distant one as well—keeps on haunting but the new does manage to resist that as well. Loyalties are different; betrayals are different. Although, the migrant conundrum remains as significant as it always was, yet we have a new issue of settlement—of coming to terms with a new identity, refusing the 'hybrid' tag. This new identity is one of the most substantial issues of this day.

Let me finish with a disclaimer. The term 'Postmodern' in the title refers strictly to a period of time. The term does not aim to capture any single theoretical space or any monolithic '–ism', but has within its agenda merely the historicized sphere in which all these texts were composed. The different articles in this book may align to certain '–isms', but the core concept attempts to establish its presence across and within the entire fabric of theorization and tries to prove that it is not confined to any single thread that has tried to dominate the identity or the movement of any people or any individual.

Siddhartha Biswas

List of Contributors

Paramita Dutta is an Assistant Professor and Head of the Department of English at Rammohan College, Baithakkhana, Kolkata. Previously, she has taught as Assistant Professor of English at Chandernagore Government College, Chandannagar, West Bengal, for more than six years. She has also taught English literature at the postgraduate level in Lady Brabourne College and Maulana Azad College, Kolkata, as a Guest Faculty.

Sharanya Dutta is an Assistant Professor at the Department of English, Kaliyaganj College, Kaliyaganj, West Bengal. He has also taught at the Postgraduate Department of English, St. Paul's Cathedral Mission College, Baithakkhana, Kolkata. He completed his M.Phil. from University of Calcutta and is now a Ph.D. scholar in the same university.

Trayee Sinha, M.Phil., Ph.D., teaches English as an Assistant Professor at Bidhan Chandra College, Asansol.

Mohona Chatterjee is doing her Ph.D. at the Department of English, West Bengal State University (W.B.S.U.), Barasat, West Bengal. She is an Assistant Professor, AIESR, Amity University, Kolkata.

Debaditya Mukhopadhyay is an Assistant Professor of English at Manikchak College, affiliated to University of Gour Banga. He is also pursuing his Ph.D. on Spy Fiction from Rabindra Bharati University, Kolkata.

Samata Biswas is an Assistant Professor at the Department of Women's Studies, Sivanath Sastri College, Kankulia, Kolkata. A trained psychologist, Dr. Biswas's areas of interest include Gender, Sexuality, Mental Health, and Psychoanalysis. She is also involved in the Diploma Course on 'Dance Movement Therapy' organized by Kolkata Sanved and the Centre for Lifelong Learning, Tata Institute of Social Sciences, as a guest faculty.

Zenith Roy, Assistant Professor at the Department of English, Dinabandhu Mahavidyalaya, Bongaon, has been associated with teaching for the last 16 years.

Susmita Paul has done her Masters from the University of Calcutta and is presently teaching English at an institution under West Bengal Board of Secondary Education. Her areas of interest are Feminist literature, African American literature, and Post-modernist literature.

Rudrashis Datta is an Assistant Professor in English at Pritilata Waddedar Mahavidyalaya, Nadia, West Bengal. He is also a guest faculty in the Post Graduate section of the Department of English, St. Paul's Cathedral Mission College, Kolkata.

Arpa Ghosh teaches literature at Vivekananda College for Women, Kolkata. She has completed two Minor Research Projects funded by the UGC—one on South African fictional strategies and the other on identity as constructed in the Bengali master-text. At the moment, she is at work on her third Minor Research Project, themed on magic realism and Salman Rushdie. She is also a short story and feature writer whose work is regularly published in the Statesman, an Indian national daily.

Pritha Kundu is an Assistant Professor in English at Hiralal Mazumdar Memorial College for Women, Dakshineswar, Kolkata. She has co-edited two books, namely *Imperial Maladies: Literatures on Medicine and Psychoanalysis in India* (jointly with Dr. Debashish Bandyopadhyay, published by Nova Publishers, USA), and *Shakespeare in Focus: In Commemoration of the Quatercentenary of Shakespeare's Death* (jointly with Dr. Debdas Roy). She is also the co-editor of *Middle Flight*, a UGC approved Peer-reviewed Journal.

Abin Chakraborty currently teaches as Assistant Professor in English at Chandernagore Government College, Chandannagar, West Bengal. He is also the editor of *Postcolonial Interventions: An Interdisciplinary Journal of Postcolonial Studies.*

Sagnik Banerjee is an Assistant Professor in English at Sundarban Hazi Desarat College, Pathankhali, West Bengal. He is also a Ph.D. Research Scholar at the Department of English, University of Calcutta.

Saikat Sarkar is an Assistant Professor at the Postgraduate Department of English, Midnapore College (Autonomous), Midnapore, West Bengal. A recipient of U.S. Department of State Fellowship, Dr. Sarkar has participated in NEH Summer Workshop at Rochester, New York, in 2011.

Nivedita Bachhar obtained her M.Phil. from University of Calcutta. She has also taught at Deshbandhu College for Girls, Kolkata, and Asutosh College, Kolkata. Currently an independent scholar residing in Manila, Philippines, her areas of interest include human rights, postmodern literature, popular culture, and the Gothic.

Rishiraj Pal is pursuing his doctoral research in modernist fiction at the Department of English and Other Modern European Languages, Visva-Bharati University, Bolpur, West Bengal. He is also a Guest Lecturer at the Postgraduate Department of English, St. Paul's Cathedral Mission College, Kolkata. In 2016, he was awarded full scholarships to attend 20th Trieste Joyce Summer School at University of Trieste, Italy, and Dublin James Joyce Summer School at University College, Dublin, Ireland.

Siddhartha Biswas is an Associate Professor in the Department of English, University of Calcutta, Kolkata. He has taught at the Department of English, St. Paul's Cathedral Mission College, for seventeen years before joining the university. His written books include *Theatre Theory and Performance* (Cambridge Scholars Publishing, U.K.) among others.

Exclusion and Migration: The De-Constructed Home

1

"What have we to do with Pakistan? We were born here": Exodus Revisited in Khushwant Singh's *Train to Pakistan*

Paramita Dutta

> And the LORD said, I have surely seen the affliction of my people which are in Egypt, and have heard their cry by reason of their taskmasters; for I know their sorrows.
>
> And I am come down to deliver them out of the hand of the Egyptians, and to bring them up out of that land unto a good land and a large, unto a land flowing with milk and honey; unto the place of the Canaanites, and the Hittites, and the Amorites, and the Perizzites, and the Hivites, and the Jebusites.
>
> Now therefore, behold, the cry of the children of Israel is come unto me: and I have also seen the oppression wherewith the Egyptians oppress them.
>
> Come now therefore, and I will send thee unto Pharaoh, that thou mayest bring forth my people the children of Israel out of Egypt.
>
> [*The Book of Exodus,* 3: 7-10; *The King James Bible*]

The later chapters of The Book of Genesis in *The Bible*, Old Testament, recount a famine in Canaan and the migration of the sons of Jacob and their clans to Egypt, where they settle under the protection of their brother Joseph, who had become the prime minister of that land. There, the Israelites multiply in large numbers and become strong.

The Book of Exodus opens around more than four hundred years after the death of Jacob, his family and the Pharaoh he served, and with a new Pharaoh, who is unaware of the historical importance of Joseph. This Pharaoh becomes concerned about the military threats and repercussions of the huge increase of the Israelite population and enslaves them and inflicts tortures and suffering on them, including the order of killing their male first born.

Atrocities continue, and finally God himself appears to Moses, who had been saved as an infant and brought up by the Pharaoh's daughter as an Egyptian prince (before he fled to Midian after killing an Egyptian and there worked and lived as a shepherd) and informs him of his plan to return the Israelites to Canaan and to send Moses back to Egypt to accomplish this task, as seen in the extract above.

What follows is the 'exodus' or 'mass departure/migration' of the Israelites from Egypt to the Promised Land, amidst many dramatic events, under the guidance of Moses, who acts on divine instructions and orders and even communicates face to face with God on Mount Sinai.

We also witness a similar exodus in Khushwant Singh's first novel *Train to Pakistan* (1956). This work has the distinction of being the first English novel to be written on the theme of the Partition of India, a veritable holocaust accompanying the nation's independence from British rule in 1947, which resulted in the mass departure of thousands, both Hindus and Muslims (as the sovereign nation-states of India and Pakistan were created on religious lines as an outcome of much political manoeuvring) and also in the violent and brutal massacre of innumerable innocents. Frances Harrison has described the events following the Partition "the largest two-way land migration in history" (94) as it uprooted hundreds of Hindus and Sikhs in Pakistan and Muslims in India and transformed them into refugees overnight. Singh had lived through the Partition and had crossed borders to India, and in this novel very concisely points out that no single religious community could be solely accused of committing violent atrocities during Partition as:

> The fact is, both sides killed. Both shot and stabbed and speared and clubbed. Both tortured. Both raped. (1)

Although the exodus of the Muslims to Pakistan in this novel, as an outcome of the Partition violence, has many resonances with the story of the migration of the Israelites to the Promised Land with Moses in the Biblical *Book of Exodus,* one needs to first discuss the novel in greater detail to understand and compare the finer nuances, similarities and differences of both the journeys that are undertaken ostensibly in search of a 'home'.

Mano Majra and its Railway Station

The novel portrays an insulated village on the Punjab border between Pakistan and India in 1947, the fictional Mano Majra, whose predominantly Sikh and Muslim inhabitants are initially shown as unaware that the British imperialists had left the country after partitioning it into India and the Muslim state of Pakistan, and consequently live in communal harmony and remain one of the few 'oases of peace' (Singh, 2) near the frontier. The place is unique in having only one Hindu family that of Ram Lal, the moneylender, who is killed by the dacoits, Malli and his gang, who come to rob him as the novel begins. The only link of Mano Majra with the outside world is its railway station.

As Mano Majra was situated right on the border of the two countries as well as on the railway route along which most of the communal violence of the Partition occurred, Frances Harrison has censured Khushwant Singh's depiction of the complete political ignorance of its people as improbable and largely arising out of Singh's desire to accentuate the political naivety of the people and depict the Partition to be a result of the despicable scheming of politicians sitting in Delhi and not a natural corollary of popular demand and cultural incompatibility (99-101).

Although Harrison's objections cannot be wholly gainsaid, Singh's representation of Mano Majra also needs to be noted:

> Not many trains stop at Mano Majra. Express trains do not stop at all. Of the many slow passenger trains, only two, one from Delhi to Lahore in the mornings and the other from Lahore to Delhi in the evenings, are scheduled to stop for a few minutes. The others stop only when they

> are held up. The only regular customers are the goods trains. (4)

Rituparna Roy, in her study of the symbolic significance of trains and the train as a lasting image of Partition in the subcontinent, had referred to Krishan Chander's short story 'Peshawar Express', where this express train had been assigned the narrator's role by the author. This train, while passing through one conflict-torn territory to another, carried not only corpses but rumours and sickening tales of the terrors of Partition violence and acquired the status of a reporter commenting on the violence rocking various parts of the nation after the Partition (35-36). In light of this role of a train during Partition, the fact that not many trains stopped in Mano Majra, whereby there could be a regular traffic of people and exchange of news and current state of affairs, could be a contributing factor towards the lack of knowledge of its inhabitants, who lived sheltered from outside harsh reality, in an idyllic world of their own. Moreover, this could at least partially undercut Harrison's objections to Singh's portrayal of the people of Mano Majra.

The political ignorance of the villagers of Mano Majra finds a parallel in the complete lack of knowledge of the electoral process and functioning of democracy of the villagers living in the Naxalite areas of the deep and conflict ridden forests of Chhattisgarh in modern day India, as depicted in a recent Hindi film called *Newton* directed by Amit V. Masurkar, where the villagers are forced to vote in spite of not having any idea of who and why they are voting for and the utility of this exercise. In one scene the character of Malko tells the presiding officer Newton how in spite of being in the same age and time, how little the outside urban world knows of the harsh realities faced by the common people of these villages located in remote interior forests. The vice versa is also true as the common people are shown to have no clue of the outside world, democracy or government and the election process have no significance for them. Utter lack of communication with the outside world leads to the ignorance of the villagers as depicted in this film, which would also be the case in *Train to Pakistan*.

The 'Ghost' Trains and Political Awakening

Khushwant Singh uses the symbol of the train, to portray how this sleepy village is rudely jolted out of its political and social slumber and made to face the reality of the Partition and its accompanying brutal violence. The first hint of the ensuing chaos comes through his description in the chapter entitled "Kalyug" of how the peaceful diurnal rhythm of the villagers is disrupted once the trains start running out of schedule:

> Early in September the time schedule in Mano Majra started going wrong. Trains became less punctual than ever before and many more started to run through at night. Some days it seemed as though the alarm clock had been set for the wrong hours. On others, it was as if no one had remembered to wind it. Imam Baksh waited for Meet Singh to make the first start. Meet Singh waited for the mullah's call to prayer before getting up. People stayed in bed late without realizing that times had changed and the mail train might not run through at all. Children did not know when to be hungry, and clamoured for food all the time. In the evenings, everyone was indoors before sunset and in bed before the express came by—if it did come by. Goods trains had stopped running altogether, so there was no lullaby to lull them to sleep. Instead, ghost trains went past at odd hours between midnight and dawn, disturbing the dreams of Mano Majra. (81)

Soon a trainload of corpses arrive from across the border and the atmosphere becomes grim and uneasy. The villagers have to arrange for the fuel to burn them. This is just the beginning of the nightmarish ordeal of the villagers. Other events follow in quick succession. Another train comes in with butchered corpses and the bodies have to be dug in a trench near the railway station. Soon the River Sutlej, merely half a mile from Mano Majra, rises and is seen to overflow with corpses of men, women and even cattle still tied to their bullock carts. Mano Majra can no longer remain insulated from the harsh reality of the Partition. Moreover, as Ralph J. Crane points out about *Train to Pakistan,* "the novel rewrites the railway, once a symbol of imperial power, as a leitmotif for Partition violence and the communal nationalism that followed the political homogenization of India and Indians during the independence struggle" (181).

The 'Othering' of the Muslims of Mano Majra

It is ironic that in spite of all the corpses that the villagers burn and bury from the trains that come across the border, the natural friendship and communal bonding between the Sikhs and Muslims in the village is shown to fall apart only because of a coldly calculated bureaucratic ploy to allegedly 'save' the Muslims. The crafty magistrate Hukum Chand, who is the mastermind of this plan, wants to evacuate the peaceful Muslims from the village especially as after the trainload of corpses arrive from Pakistan, many Sikh refugees also take shelter in the gurudwara and though the latter had not suffered any loss to person or property, Hukum Chand does not want any sort of trouble to break loose between the two groups. To that end he sows the seeds of discord between the Muslims and Sikhs in Mano Majra, by falsely insinuating that the dacoity and murder of the Hindu Lala Ram Lal in the beginning of the novel were actually committed by the Muslim Sultana and his gang (who had actually fled to Pakistan much before) and the socialist worker Iqbal was not a Sikh but a young Mussulman and a Muslim Leaguer with devious plans of his own. He even releases the actual culprits Malli and his gang and keeps imprisoned Juggut Singh and Iqbal as suspects, although the latter were innocent of this crime. His strategy succeeds and after the head constable's visit to Mano Majra following his instructions, Muslims and Sikhs begin to be polarized against each other and soon utopia dissolves into dystopia.

Singh shows how it is entirely the upshot of this administrative and political tactic that the Sikhs and Muslims begin to refashion their own sects into what Benedict Anderson has brilliantly analyzed and termed the 'imagined political community', whereby through their affinity arising from imagining as belonging to the same religion, the national imaginings occur in this novel (14-16). Such is the 'image of their communion' (*Ibid.*, 15) and 'deep horizontal comradeship' (*Ibid.*, 16) experienced alike by both members of communities that the Muslims consider the Sikhs to be 'anti-Muslim' and "For the first time, the name

Pakistan came to mean something to them—a refuge where there were no Sikhs" (Singh, 128). An atmosphere of mistrust grows between the two communities and erstwhile news of atrocities that had been ignored begins to be taken seriously. Whereas the Muslims feel "Quite suddenly, every Sikh in Mano Majra, became a stranger with an evil intent" (*Ibid.*, 128), the Sikhs decide to "be angry with the Muslims; Muslims were basely ungrateful" (*Ibid.*, 129). Soon this atmosphere leads to the 'othering' of the Muslims in their own village where they have lived for generations, and the issue of their eviction from Mano Majra, their own home.

Yet, in spite of the fact that they were seething with new found hatred for the Muslim sect, for the Sikhs, paradoxically, "Group loyalty was above reason" (*Ibid.*, 131) and they could not directly visualize throwing their own Muslim tenants out of their village (*Ibid.*, 132) reinforcing Anderson's dictum that 'nationality' or 'nation-ness' as well as nationalism are not only difficult to define but also 'cultural artefacts' (12-13).

In one of the most poignant sections of this novel, when the Sikh peasants hold a meeting at the lambardar's house at night and are at loggerheads on what is to be done about the Muslims in their village, the aged Imam Baksh enters and meekly enquires, "Well, brothers, what is your decision about us?" (Singh, 133) a query that rings full of pathos and vulnerability of a people faced with the predicament of being displaced from their own homes.

When the tearful Baksh cries ruefully, "What have we to do with Pakistan? We were born here. So were our ancestors. We have lived among you as brothers" (*Ibid.*, 133), and breaks down, the extent of the personal human tragedy of a people being suddenly divided on the basis of religion and forced to migrate from their homes and become refugees overnight, and all because of the political event of Partition, is driven home. It becomes apparent that not any intrinsic communal hatred but complex social, political and administrative reasons lead to the 'othering' of the Muslims in their own village and their consequent expulsion in the novel, forcing them to undertake a journey purportedly in search of a 'home' in Pakistan that is at its best imaginary, and in search of a sanctuary that is largely illusory.

Exodus: Purpose and Nature

As mentioned in the beginning of this paper, the exodus of the Muslims to Pakistan in this novel has quite a few resonances with the story of the migration of the Israelites to the Promised Land with Moses in the Biblical *Book of Exodus* and if we make a comparative study both journeys which involved mass migrations in search for a home, we will see that both migrations were necessity-oriented. In the *Bible*, the Israelites needed to escape the slavery of the Egyptian Pharaoh and go live in their Promised Land freely, whereas in *Train to Pakistan,* the Muslims needed to go to their own nation created specifically for them and escape the horrifying violence accompanying the Partition.

However, in the Biblical story, the land was promised to them by God who wanted to deliver them from the hands of the Egyptians, and the exodus happened because of divine intervention through the medium of Moses who was chosen to help the Israelites escape slavery and guide them to their destination. The Muslims in Singh's novel, on the other hand, were uprooted from their own lands and homes, and forced to leave in spite of not wanting to go, did not have anyone to guide them, and their migration was ordained not divinely but by the current pressures and strategies of politics and administration that used religion as a tool to further their ends.

In *The Bible*, when the Israelites left with Moses, they knew their migration was to be permanent, never to return. The Muslims and even the Sikhs in Singh's novel, however, were under the impression that the Muslims would merely be leaving for a few days to stay in the camp at Chundunnugger and return when the situation turned in their favour. When the police ask them to only take those belongings they can carry, as they would be going by train and not road to Pakistan, the news comes as a surprise to all in Mano Majra. What the Muslims had thought was a temporary journey was actually a permanent migration. After the Muslims board the trucks Singh describes:

> The officer shouted 'Pakistan!' His soldiers answered in a chorus '*Forever!*' (145) (emphasis mine)

This comes as a shock to the Muslims, who are forced to leave their belongings in the custody of the dacoit Malli and his gang (who had been released from prison), knowing very well that their material possessions would be looted by the latter and they would never regain them.

So one may emphasize that for the Israelites the escape from Egypt to the Promised Land was a step consciously undertaken, whereas the Muslims in this novel are forced to migrate as an outcome of being excluded from their community. The Muslims in this novel as happened in real life during the Partition, were made into 'refugees in their own homes' and underwent the "trauma of moving with nowhere to move" (Pandey, 2261). Radhika Chopra analyses perfectly when she says that the 'real sorrow' of the partition was that it "brought to an abrupt end a long and communally shared history and cultural heritage" (164), what we witness in *Train to Pakistan.*

Conclusion

It has been said that 'independence is an abstract thing' but "partition was 'in a negative sense' a very tangible reality" (Pandey, 2261). That is exactly what we see in this novel, when Iqbal, the socialist worker, who comes to Mano Majra, realizes that "Independence meant little or nothing to these people" who were common villagers mired in poverty (Singh, 51). Political freedom could be a concrete reality to only those who were first economically independent and secure. The unnamed Muslim sums up the common man's understanding of the Independence struggle of India and its accompanying Partition in an analysis that is startling and disheartening but cannot entirely be overridden:

> Freedom is for the educated people who fought for it. We were slaves of the English, now we will be slaves of the educated Indians—or the Pakistanis. (Singh, 52)

Defeating the entire purpose of the sacrifice of millions for the struggle for Indian Independence, Banta Singh utters grimly, "We were better off under the British. At least there was security" (*Ibid.*, 53) especially as they would not get 'more lands or more buffaloes' (*Ibid.*, 51) out of this newly found freedom and nor were they educated enough to get jobs. Ideology or lofty political discourse, it is shown, cannot be either comprehended or practised in an empty stomach.

But the partition and the indiscriminate, stomach churning mob violence accompanying it, directly affected people, and disrupted the communal harmony of the Sikhs and Muslims, and forced the latter to leave their homes in search of another home in another land not known to them in the hope of a largely imaginary security. Historically, the Muslims who went from India to Pakistan, were distinguished from those originally living in Pakistan by the appellation of *Muhajir* (Khalidi, 242), and looked down upon which goes on to show what kind of a 'home' they found in Pakistan.

Religion, which was the foundation of the Partition of India, and culminated in the two way migration of Hindus and Muslims across the borders of India and Pakistan, is also reduced to external markers such as circumcision, bangles on the hand, length of hair and names in this novel. Hence the confusion surrounding the socialist worker whose name is given only as Iqbal, who can either be Sikh (Iqbal Singh), Hindu (Iqbal Chand) or Muslim (Iqbal Mohammad/Mohammad Iqbal); who wears a bangle on his right hand like a Sikh but unlike one does not sport long hair and is clean-shaven; and moreover is circumcised like a Muslim. The indeterminacy of these markers makes his identity slippery and lands Iqbal in serious trouble.

Khushwant Singh seems to imply that if religion is merely viewed as not spiritual awakening and relationship with god, but a series of factors extrinsic to faith or belief, then its signs become fluid and exchangeable, which can be easily impersonated by those belonging to other religions and this defeats the entire purpose of the Partition or dividing nations on rigidly religious lines. The recent Rajkumar Hirani film called *PK* voices this same problem of associating external markers such as dress with religion in a comic episode where the alien protagonist dresses up people of different religious communities in each other's outfits and asks the fundamentalist Guru Tapasvi Maharaj to identify the individual person's religion. Associating the external markers of dress and other accessories with an internal belief system he fails completely in identifying the correct religions of the people of different communities. This episode gives a very important message of communal harmony, love and peace, that of people of all religions being essentially the same, however, different may be their faiths or beliefs. In *Train to Pakistan* too, communal harmony in Mano Majra was ingrained, and the friction arose out of factors not religious, but political, which ultimately contributed to the mass exodus of the people.

One may conclude by saying that in the Biblical story, God directly helped in protecting the Israelites from the armies of the Egyptian Pharaoh by drowning the latter in the Red Sea, after he had parted it only for his chosen people to escape. In this novel, it is one from the community of Sikhs, the perpetrators of the plot to kill the Muslims, the 'badmash' Juggut Singh/Jugga who is redeemed by the power of love for the Muslim Nooran who is in the train and acts heroically to foil the plans of the other Sikhs that the Muslims are saved from being massacred. Jugga dies but his goal that the Muslims in the train to Pakistan should cross the border unharmed is assured:

> The rope had been cut in shreds. Only a thin tough strand remained. He went at it with the knife, and then with his teeth. The engine was almost on him. There was a volley of shots. The man shivered and collapsed. The rope snapped in the centre as he fell. The train went over him, and went on to Pakistan. (Singh, 190)

Juggut Singh's act of cutting off the rope stretched across the bridge becomes a "moment which expels the Muslims even as it saves them" (Ralph J. Crane, 192), and one can view the exodus of the Muslims at the end, as ultimately a flight to freedom from mob violence, and a journey for life, for a home, however unconscious it may be and illusive the quest might seem.

Postscript

Unfortunately, history has the habit of repeating itself in various forms, and as this paper is being written, in the global scene today, the world is witnessing a similar exodus of Rohingya Muslims from Myanmar, where their community is facing exclusion and torture from the majority Buddhist population, resulting in their forced migration to Bangladesh and India to protect their lives and in the hope, however intangible, of finding a home.

Works Cited

Anderson, Benedict. *Imagined Communities: Reflections on the Origin and Spread of Nationalism.* London: Verso, 1983. Print.

Chopra, Radhika. "Partitioned Lives in Khushwant Singh's *Train to Pakistan* and Manju Kapur's *Difficult Daughters*". *Indian Literature* 54.3 (2010): 164-175. JStor. Web. 20 December 2015.

Crane, Ralph J. "Inscribing a Sikh India: An Alternative Reading of Khushwant Singh's *Train to Pakistan*". *Cross Cultures: Readings in the Post/Colonial Literatures in English, Vol. 82. Alternative Indias: Writing, Nation and Communalism.* Ed. Peter Morey and Alex Tickell. Amsterdam, NLD: Editions Rodopi, 2005. 181-96. ProQuest Ebrary. Web. 19 December 2015.

Gopal, Priyamvada. *Indian English Novel: Nation, History and Narration.* Oxford, GBR: Oxford University Press, 2009. ProQuest Ebrary. Web. 20 December 2015.

Harrison, Frances. "Literary Representation: Partition in Indian and Pakistani Novels in English." *Indian Literature* 34.5 (1991): 94-110. JStor. Web. 20 December 2015.

Khalidi, Omar. "From Torrent to Trickle: Indian Muslim Migration to Pakistan, 1947-97". *Islamic Studies* 37.3 (1998): 339-52. JStor. Web. 20 December 2015.

King James Bible: The Preserved and Living Word of God. https://www.kingjamesbibleonline.org/. 22 September 2017.

Newton. Dir. Amit V. Masurkar. Perf. Rajkumar Rao, Pankaj Tripathi, Anjali Patil, Raghubir Yadav. Drishyam Films, 2017. Film.

Pandey, Gyanendra. "Partition and Independence in Delhi: 1947-48". *Economic and Political Weekly* 32.36 (1997): 2261-72. JStor. Web. 20 December 2015.

PK. Dir. Rajkumar Hirani. Perf. Aamir Khan, Anushka Sharma, Sanjay Dutt, Boman Irani, Saurabh Shukla and Sushant Singh Rajput. Vidhu Vinod Chopra Films; Rajkumar Hirani Films, 2014. Film.

Roy, Rituparna. *South Asian Partition Fiction in English: From Khushwant Singh to Amitav Ghosh.* Amsterdam, NLD: Amsterdam University Press, 2010. ProQuest Ebrary. Web. 20 December 2015.

Singh, Khushwant. *Train to Pakistan.* Gurgaon, India: Penguin Books India and Ravi Dayal Publisher, 2009. Print.

2

Making a Journey and Resisting It: Ambiguity and Paradox in Kazuo Ishiguro's *A Pale View of Hills*

Sharanya Dutta

It is difficult to think of a work of fiction without any 'journey' taking place in it, if the signifier in question stands not only for physical movement but also for metaphorical change of state. Therefore, it is no surprise that Kazuo Ishiguro's *A Pale View of Hills* (1982) depicts a number of journeys. This paper seeks to investigate the pattern that emerges from the interaction of those journeys—often overlapping, often nullifying one another through contradiction and thus leading to ambiguity as well as paradox. A convenient point of entry to the complex pattern should be the fact that the novel is structured around two journeys—Sachiko's journey to America and Etsuko's journey to England. Both these journeys, as it appears from the names of concrete destinations, are physical in nature.

However, there is a remarkable divergence between these two journeys that will not escape even the most casual reader. We are told all about the circumstances of Sachiko's journey but remain unsure whether she actually accomplishes it or not. She is seen making repeated attempts to make the journey possible and having repeated failures in doing so. She has an alternative location in mind, too: her uncle's house. The hypothetical journeys are hardly comparable in magnitude: while America is too distant and too unknown, her uncle's house is too nearby and too familiar. She oscillates between these two journeys and, when she finally leaves, we do not know which journey she has actually undertaken. Interestingly, her presence in the novel simply asserts the need of making a journey—a journey which is undefined, uncertain and unrealistic. On the other hand, her daughter Mariko embodies something that is the greatest barrier for a journey: obsession. It is her obsession with her kittens that resists Sachiko's ambition of moving to a better place. For an adult, however, such a childish resistance is meaningless and necessitates violence, nothing but violence.

The other important journey is Etsuko's. We simply know that the journey has taken place. But the detailing of its circumstances is—perhaps deliberately—withdrawn. This is diametrically opposite to Sachiko's journey where detailing is prioritized over surety. In all likelihood, the two journeys contrast and complement each other. If we need the detailing of circumstances, we have Sachiko's journey. If we need the surety that the journey has really occurred, we have Etsuko's. These two may serve as two aspects of the same journey, if we think of their combined effect. At the same time, these two may also serve to show that no two journeys are same, thereby contributing to the framework of multi-layered journeys.

Rather than focusing on the journey itself, the novel shows a part of Etsuko's life a few years before the journey and another part a few years after it. These two parts are separated not only by time but also by geographical distance. The earlier part is set in Japan and the later part, in England. To state the obvious, Etsuko herself is the common thread between these two different times and places. Though there is a gap about which we are told absolutely nothing, everything before and after it seems to form a continuum. A literary work that portrays the migration of its protagonist (Bharati Mukherjee's *Jasmine*, for instance) usually emphasizes on the metamorphosis which such a journey can bring about. Here, Etsuko has miraculously managed to remain the same, adding an element of paradox.

The paradox stems from our desire to find a meaning in a journey, often epitomized in the form of the construction of a different identity. Because identity is understood in terms of a location, a shift in the latter is supposed to bring about a shift in the former. Ordinarily the shift operates along the syntagmatic axis of identity and we have to deduce the paradigmatic from the alternative possibilities of the journey itself. The challenge in interpreting Etsuko's fixation lies primarily in finding out whether or not it entails Etsuko's active participation—in other words, whether or not she chooses to remain static. On one level, she is a passive observer, a recorder of facts and impressions, who lacks the psychological malleability to get moulded by her change of situation. But, on another level, much of her alienation is clearly self-inflicted and the construction of a new identity intentionally, even forcibly, resisted.

The novel's complete silence regarding Etsuko's journey serves to blur its facts and to shape it into a nameless, faceless, vacuous presence. Etsuko being the protagonist, hers must be the most important journey in the novel. So, it may appear somewhat puzzling that the novel leaves it entirely to the reader's speculation, not even giving any number of hints from which one may form a conjecture. Perhaps Japan and England are represented more as mental spaces than geographical locations. Or perhaps the forced nature of the journey has not been able to tear out the older location from the persona of the protagonist. That may explain why the corporeality of the journey has been deliberately undermined. Therefore, trying to establish a link between Etsuko's present and her past by means of a well-defined journey is epistemologically non-viable.

While we do not and perhaps should not see Etsuko making her journey from Japan to England, we nevertheless see her in the process of making a journey in the opposite direction. This is not a physical journey but a journey of her memory. As we regularly find in the fiction of migration, the memory of the protagonist is a very important tool which can juxtapose different times and places. In Etsuko's case, however, the juxtaposition is incomplete, as is her migration. She is a person who almost lives in her past. We always have the feeling that she is in the post-war Japan even though we know she is in the England of the 80s. Her current location is purely incidental, a product of logistic convenience. Mentally, she is still in her own land, loyal to her old self and old identity. This creates a split in the supposedly unified entity of her character, or, to be more precise, a split in our construction of the migrant character.

Though it is certainly provoked by Keiko's suicide, Etsuko's memory does not travel back to Keiko's childhood. Instead, it travels back to the time when she was pregnant with Keiko and having regular communication with Sachiko and Mariko. The character of Keiko has not been developed in the traditional sense. We have only fragments—bits and pieces—from which we can speculate an individual at odds with her situation. As we see everything through Etsuko's camera lens, this fragmentary representation of Keiko reflects Etsuko's fragmentary understanding. Keiko belongs to the new world from which Etsuko has always maintained a distance. She has always been unable and unwilling to understand it. This lack of empathy from the mother figure may be one of the reasons why Keiko ultimately takes her own life. Whatever the immediate cause of her suicide, it is obvious that her restless suffering originates from generational conflict. She *is* the England of the 80s while her mother *is* the post-war Japan. Without getting into the details of this conflict, the novel highlights the characters of Sachiko and Mariko, who, in a traditional analysis of fiction, should be regarded as minor characters. But Sachiko is actually an extension of Etsuko's self and Mariko, Keiko's. By creating a double parallelism the novel effectively strengthens its journey motif.

At the most basic, the image of a journey is represented by Etsuko's walk through the wasteground. The wasteground may symbolize everything that heaths have symbolized in English literature. It may also be the entire Nagasaki in a semantic microcosm, evoking traumatic echoes of the war. Significantly, this piece of land lies between Etsuko's apartment and Sachiko's cottage. One is tempted to interpret this as a sign that the distance between them, though traversable, is barren and futile. This serves as the model for longer journeys as well. Etsuko's journey to England does not seem to have produced any transformational impact other than her total surrender to her memories.

We have the grotesque image of the murder of Mariko's kittens in the form of a journey by water. We notice her obsession with her kittens in passages like the following:

> "How did you spend your day today, Mariko?" I asked. "Did you do any drawing?"
>
> "I played with Atsu and Mee-Chan."
>
> "That's nice. And where do they live? Are they from the apartments?"
>
> "That's Atsu"—she pointed to one of the small black kittens beside her—"and that's Mee-Chan."
>
> "But you should try and make friends with the other children. I'm sure they're all very nice."
>
> "They stole Suji-Chan. He was my favourite kitten."
>
> "They stole him? Oh dear, I wonder why they did that."
>
> Mariko began stroking a kitten. "I've lost Suji-Chan now."
>
> "Perhaps he'll turn up soon. I'm sure the children were just playing."
>
> "They killed him. I've lost Suji-Chan now."
>
> "Oh, I wonder why they did a thing like that."
>
> "I threw stones at them. Because they said things."
>
> "Well, you shouldn't throw stones, Mariko."
>
> "They said things. About Mother. I threw stones at them and they took Suji-Chan and wouldn't give him back." (79)

Here we do not know whether Mariko's accusation is correct or not. But in a later passage—one of the most shocking in the novel—her mother actually kills the remaining kittens by drowning them:

> Sachiko brought her hands out of the water and stared at the kitten she was still holding. She brought it closer to her face and the water ran down her wrists and arms.
>
> "It's still alive," she said, tiredly. Then she turned to me and said: "Look at this water, Etsuko. It's so dirty." With an air of disgust, she dropped the soaked kitten back into the box and shut it. "How these things struggle," she muttered, and held up her wrists to show me the scratch-marks. [...]

> Sachiko adjusted her position then pushed the vegetable box over the edge of the bank; the box rolled and landed in the water. To prevent it floating, Sachiko leaned forward and held it down. The water came almost halfway up the wire-grid. She continued to hold down the box, then finally pushed it with both hands. The box floated a little way into the river, bobbed and sank further. Sachiko got to her feet, and we both of us watched the box. It continued to float, then caught in the current and began moving more swiftly downstream. (167-68)

The vegetable box in which the kittens are drowned is actually the prize of a lottery in which Mariko participated. It was a pleasant day for the three of them—Etsuko, Sachiko and Mariko—as they travelled in different parts of Nagasaki and gathered various experiences. It is the only instance in the novel where journeys are depicted in vivid detail. We have the description of their travel by ropeways and later by tram. These journeys are apparently trivial: they do not cause any significant change in the lives of the main characters. Still, these have been described at length. In contrast, more important journeys have been omitted. It is part of the novel's strategy to show that memory sometimes brings back trivial things at the expense of serious ones. In fact, these experiences and journeys are specimens of the locational paradox. The old cannot be sustained and the new cannot be accepted. Unlike Ogata-San, Etsuko does not glamorize or romanticize her past. She is fully aware of the squalor that her past consists of. Still, she is trapped within it. Her "[w]andering between two worlds, one dead, [t] he other powerless to be born" foregrounds the problem of dislocation. She knows that the old world is no longer fit to live in from practical perspectives. Therefore, she is forced to become a migrant. But she is extremely reluctant to sacrifice the essential identity of the old land. If anything, her character is a recursive utterance of this dilemma.

There are two important visits in the novel—one by Ogata-San in Etsuko's past and the other by Niki in Etsuko's present. Ogata-San is a character who finds it difficult to come to terms with the new generation and lives in a world that is oblivious to change. He reminds us of Shūkichi Hirayama in Yasujirō Ozu's 1953 film *Tokyo Story*. Ogata-San believes in certain values, very much feudal in nature, which seem to have lost their relevance in the 'new', capitalistic Japan. Nowhere is it more obvious than in the episode of his encounter with his once favourite student, Shigeo Matsuda. Here we have a situation of conflict, we expect nothing less than a tremendous explosion but all we have is a formal exchange of words. The old world is too overwhelmed to find an appropriate expression, the new world is too confident that it has already replaced the old world and does not need to exert itself any further.

Niki's visit, too, is extremely important because it enables Etsuko to understand what a drastic change has taken place. Unlike Ogata-San, she does not overreact or try to impose her own views on her daughter. It seems that she, though doubtful of the changing paradigm, has made peace with it. First, she is different from Ogata-San as an individual. Second, she has witnessed a huge number of changes already. Therefore, she does not demand unwavering faith to monolithic ideals. She makes an attempt to comprehend the world of her daughter. But her daughter does not do the same thing with respect to her. We can say that Etsuko is more balanced than both Ogata-San and Niki. It is surprising how these two characters, having almost nothing in common, share a peculiar stubbornness in the belief that his or her generation has the final word for everything.

The idea of adjustment through negation/nostalgia is a powerful motif in this novel. It also shows the failure of adjustment from the apparently adjusted. Keiko's suicide is a case in point. The senior figure fails to understand the new and the anxieties of the next generation adapting within the new.

By bringing together people from different generations, the novel illustrates that journeys are largely ineffective in reducing distances. Language itself seems static. It makes no journey from one mind to another as it is supposed to do. Still, journeys are always considered important. The reason probably lies in the impact that a journey has on a person's individual identity. Often a journey, however futile it might be, serves as the instrument for self-expression as well as self-assertion. One needs to have the feeling that one is making a journey. Its ontology is as irrelevant as its teleology: all that matters is its taking place at all.

Journeys in this novel are variations of the Beckettian waiting: we are moving from one location to another with the vague idea that we are going to achieve something. That hope is what keeps us alive. Even though we have innumerable experiences and we know how unfeasible our hopes generally are, we tend to think of each journey as one in a series of trial-and-errors and move on to the next. While Sachiko gives us a glaring example of this particular aspect of a journey, Etsuko, too, exemplifies it in a much more subtle way. The fact that trauma follows wherever one may go is a key factor for both of them.

The phrase 'pale view' in the title of the novel is quite significant. Things of the past, filtered by human memory, offer only a pale view. But here Etsuko is living in the past and has a more prominent view of her 'then' than her 'now'. So, in this case, the pale view may refer to her present. This argument may be refuted by pointing out that 'Hills' are more abundant in Japan than in England. But the title, in all probability, is heterotopic. Any attempt to reduce it to the convenience of a single space would miss the nuances of the journey motif.

The interplay of time is crucial in understanding the significance of journeys. Usually we think of a journey as a spatial shift, but the temporal shift is equally, if not more, important. In the context of this novel, journeys are associated with generational change, as we have already seen. However, all the characters in this novel are flat: they hardly make any inward journey from immaturity to maturity, or from one set of ideals to another. But, through the changing paradigm, the community itself is making an enormous journey—from the horrors of war to the stability of peace, from tyranny to democracy, from family values to individualism, from obedience to ambition. All we are left with is a complete fragmentation of the established structure. The pre- and post-journey scenarios complement each other and do not really give us the portrayal of a solution. The loss of home here is so complete that no new home can be established.

Works Cited

Gurnham, David. *Memory, Imagination, Justice*. Farnham: Ashgate, 2009. Print.

Ishiguro, Kazuo. *A Pale View of Hills*. New York: Vintage Books, 1990. Print.

Walder, Dennis. *Postcolonial Nostalgias: Writing, Representation and Memory*. New York: Routledge, 2010. Print.

3

From Bangladesh to Brick Lane: Leaving the Home in Search of a New World

Trayee Sinha

Identity formation is the part and parcel of literary discourse. One's identity can be built in different ways—one of them is to travel to gather knowledge and thus making a space of one's own. History bears the significance that travelling had become a quest motif and it has haunted people irrespective of gender, caste, class and race. The purpose of travel may be manifold, but what comes as an essential agenda is to develop one's sense of being akin in respect to different geographical settings. Home is a fixed space and it develops one's mental construction with the sense of belonging. Leaving one's own home and going to a different location may create a sense of insecurity as well as loss for some. But for the others it may create a new sense of belonging. The shift of home may create the sense of dislocation, immigration and also identity crisis. The present article attempts to explore the shift of home through travel in relation to identity formation by the analysis of Monica Ali's novel *Brick Lane*. According to Rosemary George, the primary connotation of 'home' is of the 'private' space from which the individual travels into the larger arenas of life and to which he or she returns at the end of the day. Home is also an imagined location that can be fixed in a mental landscape.

Monica Ali's novel examines the journey Nazneen makes from her native home to the strange world of Brick Lane. Nazneen becomes Ali's female immigrant subject and through her Ali represents how the South-Asian women cope up with the problems of re-constructing selfhood and the South-Asian

British identity. It was quite difficult for a girl like Nazneen's background to make a journey from Dhaka to Brick Lane—a strange land. For Nazneen who was married to a much older man, Chanu and who did not have the voice to say something, was bound to accept Brick Lane and the life over there. To her, home works as a mental image which becomes primarily a psychological construction built from the incomplete odds and ends of memory that survive from the past. The new location where she arrives through travelling is a place of necessity for her husband. She does not know English in the way the people of Brick Lane used to communicate and the absence of language is the main cause of her isolation. It may raise questions for a writer like Monica Ali who left war-tormented Dhaka in 1971 when she was barely 7 years old. She was, like Nazneen, fluent in Bengali, but after boarding the plane she claimed that she had lost the language while growing up in the northern mill town of Bolton.

Has the same thing happened to Nazneen? Since Ali is a part of the same culture of Nazneen, is she trying to find out the similarities and differences of dislocating one's self? Is she, becoming a migrant like Nazneen, tries to ask her 'self' whether a migrant is excluded and forced to look for a new home? Nazneen migrated because of her husband's purpose, she has no personal choice. Similarly, Ali left Dhaka with her family at a much earlier phase of her life when people are not in a stage to make of choice of his/her own. Going back to the odyssey of women writers in colonial Bengal, one could think of Krishnabhabini Das who gave an account of her travel in *England e Bangamahila*. But it had a different purpose which would suit her personal wish—to travel in a foreign land to come into touch with their culture. Young Nazneen may not have got the chance in a same manner, but she could make a choice out of that only at the end of the novel.

There are different layers in Nazneen's character: her culture shock of being in a new country, her trauma of losing her infant son.

Ali was greatly moved by Naila Kabeer's book *The Power to Choose* (that contains case-studies about Bangladeshi women garment workers in Dhaka and the East End of London) while plotting *Brick Lane*. The time when Ali was growing up is a phase of the gradual expansion of women's agency. Quite naturally she started being a part of this discourse and took much interest to know about women who were the underdogs but who wanted to do something of their own. This is one of the possible reasons she started taking interest to study about the different occupations of the Bangladeshi immigrants at Brick Lane—especially to know about the nature of women's work. In her writing "Where I'm Coming From" she shares some of her thoughts about *Brick Lane*:

> I could set lines of enquiry about my book (Brick Lane) into broad camps. 'Tell us about them,' is one.... The other reaction is rather different. What gives you the right to write about 'us' when you are clearly one of 'them'.... But the 'two camp' split in my case brings me back to the idea of the periphery. How can I write about a community to which I do not truly belong? Perhaps, my answer is I can write about it, because I do not truly belong. Growing up with an English mother and Bengali father means never being an insider. (Ali, 292)

Sukdev Sandhu has made a significant comment about Brick Lane. According to him

> *Brick Lane* has always been a holding area, a temporary interzone for immigrants who have not yet fully settled in England; whose lives are defined by the past—their own or that of their parents—but who wish to seize the future; who wish to become consumers rather than hunch-backed toilers. It's a slow and incomplete journey as far as many Bangladeshi's are concerned. (*London Review of Books*)

Brick Lane has several autobiographical touches and the chief of them being Ali's dislocation. Following Sandhu's words, one can follow that Brick Lane is such a space which holds the hopes and disappointments of the underprivileged immigrants. Ali's concern here is the re-construction of the female self and here she has made a departure from the traditional storyline. In this world women find it always challenging to make their separate establishment. Nazneen, the protagonist, representative of the South Asian struggling woman, asserts her views and tries to find an establishment in her new Brick Lane home. Both Ali and Nazneen left Gouripur, their ancestral village. Being a diasporic writer Ali might have occupied either a kind of 'second space' of exile and cultural solitude or it would be Bhaba's 'third space' which would signify a hybrid location of antagonism, perpetual tension and chaos. This notion of hybridity is a part of both Nazneen and Ali's life because both of them migrated and had to adopt a new culture. The perpetual tension can be explained in terms of the communal riots in Dhaka, which made Ali's family leave their native land. Brick Lane and the Bengali community over there also had similar tensions and there has been a constant dialectic shown between the values of East and the West.

Nazneen's departure to Brick Lane and her attempt to adopt British customs state her purpose—she went there for Chanu's prospect but now tries to adopt the new culture so that she may develop a new identity. Her staying at home was the source of her monotony and to get out of it she made friends over there. At the same time, the feeling of native home was somehow to be replaced by the diasporic home, which she was bound to accept first but later on she intentionally wanted to be a part of it. Ali's novel shows the development of Brick Lane as part of Anglo-Indian cuisine and many countries including Bangladesh migrated to London to look for jobs. The cuisine of Bengal has always been the part and parcel of world cuisine and Ali is making it evident at Brick Lane. It is Nazneen who cooks and delivers them, thus making the take away business lucrative. That at least gave her a pretext to become engaged in work. Chanu made her busy with two daughters and the household chores, to him, what else could she ask for? But Nazneen's new home made her think of her choice, which made her bold enough to pursue a relationship with Karim; a young man from her community.

It is also significant to note that Nazneen and thousands of women like her, although attempting to come into contact with the new culture, finally fails to perpetuate them. It is part of the concept that a Third World country like Bangladesh is still interpreted by the British in quite stereotypical a manner—it is bleak, chaotic and unmanageable and there are poor and hungry people. Such a negative stereotype is developed by the British people and the same negative image is not overlooked by Ali as part of her *Brick Lane* project. Nazneen can never be a part of this new culture but she could attempt to make the ice-skating possible which would give her a new flavour of liberation.

Ali, while dwelling on the theme of the dilemma between the native home and the diasporic home, points out an individual's isolation in terms of language. Nazneen's sister, Hasina's letters try to establish a contact between Dhaka and Brick Lane, but it could only alienate her because of the bizarre English:

> I so happy now I almost scared. Hardly dare opening my eye. Why it is?... God not putting me on earth only to suffer.... Malek go out early in the morning and coming back late late. He not knowing much about trains and such like but he say too also that do not matter. Nobody smarter than my husband. (Ali, 25)

On the other hand, it also establishes a point of similarity when the author describes the first time of Nazneen getting lost in the Brick Lane area "without a coat, without a suit, without a white face, without a destination" (52) and Hasina's condition of being lost in the web because she has lost her husband. Both the sisters in separate geographical locations suffer from the same crisis. The newly immigrated Nazneen feels alienated first for her being lost and Hasina felt alienated because of her subversion—she gets tortured by her husband and finally elopes with a cook. The only means of communication between the two sisters was epistolary after Nazneen leaves Dhaka. She tried to connect with her native home though the exchange of letters with her sister.

The people from Bengal started residing in the Tower Hamlets from 1920s onwards for various purposes. People came from Sylhet to Tower Hamlet to work for the East India Company. Ali is talking about Tower Hamlets in the 1980s when most of the people from Bangladesh went there in search of various jobs of which restaurant business was a flourishing one. Probably this is the reason of considering Brick Lane as Banglatown. Festivals such as Boishakhi Mela, Brick Lane curry festival give the essence of Bengal. Ali has maintained this tradition while portraying Nazneen who was good in cooking. She is involved in takeaway business to meet the expenses of the family on one hand and to pay the debt of Mrs. Islam on the other.

The culture of the Tower Hamlets could not wipe out the chaos and squalor of Dhaka. Although Chanu made repeated attempts to refer to Bengali culture, history, the song of Bengal; the native inhabitants of Tower Hamlets develop the same sort of bleak and snobbish attitude for those immigrants of Dhaka. Chanu's false sense of class superiority and racial ideology is expressed in his strange world of Brick Lane

> to a white person, we are all the same: dirty little monkey all in the same monkey clan. (*Brick Lane*, 21)

Without knowing the whereabouts of the immigrants staying at Brick Lane for quite a long time, Chanu superciliously talks about how most of the residents of Tower Hamlets are Sylhetis who are nothing but close minded peasants.

The series of letters written to Nazneen by her sister Hasina at regular intervals—1988 May, September, November; 1989 January, July, August, September, and the years follow—time to time Nazneen was informed of the condition of Dhaka—the chaos, the hartals, the rally of the university students. She also talks of the politicians of Dhaka who hire goons to win the elections. Men are lynched on the street. Hasina asks Nazneen:

> Sister what is happen to police and court and thing? In England could such thing happen like this? (*Brick Lane*, 221)

Nazneen, in search of her new home, got up everyday and felt

> Six months now since she'd been sent away to London. Every morning before she opened her eyes she thought, if I were the wishing type, I know what I would wish. And then she opened her eyes and saw Chanu's puffy face on the pillow next to her.... Was it cheating? To think, I know what I would wish? Was it not the same as making the wish? (*Brick Lane*, 18)

One living away from the native land always tries to get the flavour of the 'native space' and Nazneen was not an exception to this. But the memory gets blurred as time goes on and she has personally experienced that. In search of her new home

> The village was leaving her. Sometimes a picture would come. Vivid; so strong she could smell it. More often, she tried to see and could not. It was as if the village was caught up in a giant fisherman's net and she was pulling at the fine mesh with bleeding fingers, squinting into the sun, vision mottled with netting and eyelashes. As the years passed, the layers of netting multiplied and she began to rely on a different kind of memory. The memory of things she knew but no longer saw. (*Brick Lane*, 217)

On the contrary, after many years of her arrival at Brick Lane, Nazneen could feel the change of outlook in relation to her search for the new home. She accompanied Razia to Wentworth Street to buy clothes and what she could experience is the following:

> Market stalls lined the road selling leather goods, coats of every kind of synthetic, bright handbags on cheap chains, shoes that looked disposable, Jamaican patties, tinned food at 40 percent off. They ignored the stalls and stuck to the pavement. Past Regency Textiles and Excelsior Textiles Ltd, cloth draped on wire hangers in windows, Balinese prints, wax-block African prints (with certificate of authenticity), beyond the exclusive luggage of Regal Stores, past the untitled window where cellophane wrapped blocks of fabric were suspended on end in a pattern of diamonds. (*Brick Lane*, 308-09)

Views of knickknacks could provide her ideas of different fabrics and textures and give her a new vision of the fashion and textile industry far away from Dhaka; to her the sartorial fashion was something different from the place she lived in her early childhood. This could also expand her horizon. It would give her a vision which she has not had before. The change of her home has given her the expansion of mental horizon. In relation to this Nazneen's ideologies also transformed—both political, social, sexual. It is the manifestation of her shift—from her familiar native land to an unknown territory full of uncertainties. Her constant interaction and confrontation with such uncertainties made her aware of her new circumstances.

As far as the sexual and political ideologies are concerned, women, irrespective of any society are still the victims of patriarchy. They do not have a wish of their own. Nazneen suffers the same fate. She was married earlier, according to her father's wishes, not knowing about her 'choice' of husband. She was married to a much older person, Chanu who could not be of a match for her. It was not the end. Women of Nazneen's background could not dream of practicing sexuality outside marriage. Regarding political ideologies Nazneen did not have any. Perhaps Ali has intentionally done this because of the hesitation felt after the bombing of the World Trade Centre. It increases the growing difficulties of Islamic immigrants in countries like Britain. Ali's novel works as a subversive representation of a South-Asian woman breaking the taboos of Islamic tradition and developing her sexual and political ideology only when she steps outside her 'home' and immigrates to a place like Brick Lane. At 18 she comes to Brick Lane with her husband and at 34 she had an affair with Karim.

Nazneen's first encounter with ice-skating is the most captivating of her experiences in the novel. This gives her the sense of autonomy and most interestingly it is something which transforms her idea of leaving Brick Lane. Chanu decides to go back to Dhaka. But that could not change Nazneen's mind. The female ice-skater inspired her; she felt the sense of female agency from the televised image of the skater. It is like she started imagining herself in place of that skater and

> She stopped dead and flung her arms above her head with a look so triumphant that you knew she had conquered everything: her body, the laws of nature and the heart of the tight suited man, who slid over on his knees, vowing to lay down his life for her. (*Brick Lane*, 29)

She was fascinated by the skating to such an extent that it started appearing in her dreams. Nazneen tries out different western outfits and the final thing she tries out is the ice-skater's outfit

> if she had a tiny, tiny skirt with knickers to match and a tight bright top then she would—how could she not?—skate through life with a sparkling smile and a handsome man who took her hand and made her spin, spin, spin? (297)

Nazneen could see the image of a successful career woman through the female ice-skater—it is very much a part of her coming to Brick Lane because when she left Dhaka, female emancipation have not extended its roots. So it is absolutely the mobility—a taking off from her home to a new world where she could see the possibilities of female agency. At the end of the novel she paves the way to her re-construction of the self. Chanu wants to go back to Dhaka but Nazneen felt reluctant. What she has gained living in Brick Lane from her experiences is the sense of mobility. She fights against Mrs. Islam, the underground moneylender without Chanu's support. It increased her level of confidence. In addition to this she refuses Karim's marriage proposal. She made a bold attempt to go beyond the marital knot to get rid of her boredom but finally she could dissuade Karim. The borders have created differences in her mental horizon. That is why even finding Karim a worthier man than Chanu; Nazneen could make it a choice to leave Karim. Now she could feel that she can take her own decisions and live a life of her own. She gains self-awareness, independence and has the opportunity to live with the support of a female community.

At one point Yasmin Hussain critiques Brick Lane. She shows that the "novel fails to present interactions between the Bengalis and other migrant groups: the indigenous population is also conspicuously absent from the text" (Hussain, 100). She also made the following observation:

> *Brick Lane* presents an image of Britain's Bangladeshi community which is a textbook definition and it is not a book which is written from within the community it explores. (Hussain, 92)

When Monica Ali was making researches on Brick Lane she came through various experiences, one of them being observing the South Asian women's struggle to establish her separate identity. In *Brick Lane,* she has also portrayed a world where women attempt to find a place of her own. It is significant to note that in one of her interviews Monica Ali acknowledged that fact that she has no specific idea of home and that is the biggest critique of Ali's novel because in Brick Lane her protagonist shares the idea of home. Nazneen's alienation at Brick Lane works as an antidote to make her self-reliant—she can take the decision that she could survive here without her husband. It is the strange land which could finally give her the flavour to leave Chanu to fulfill her choice—it is also an indication of her victory—her reluctance to leave her native home at that point of time. But now Nazneen feels reluctant to leave Brick Lane—thus she has made up this entire journey of leaving home in search of a new world.

Works Cited

Ali, Monica. *Brick Lane*. Croydon: Blackswan, 2003. Print.

Hussain, Yasmin. *Writing Diaspora: South Asian Women, Culture and Ethnicity*. UK: Ashgate, 2005. Print.

Parameswaran, Uma. "Contextualising Diasporic Locations in Deepa Mehta's *Fire* and Srinivas Krishna's *Masala*" in *Diaspora: Theorists, Histories, Texts*. Ed. Makarand Paranjape. New Delhi: Indialog, 2001. pp. 290-300. Print.

Sandhu, Sukdev. "Come Hungry, Leave Edgy" in *London Review of Books*. 10-13. Print. Viewed on 25.05.2017.

4

Ashima and Alienation in Jhumpa Lahiri's *The Namesake*: From Myth to Modernity

Mohona Chatterjee

Ebar Amar Uma Ele
Ar Uma Re Pathabo Na
Bole Boluk Loke Mondo
Karor Kotha Shunbo Na

[This year when daughter Uma comes
I won't send her back to Kailash
Let the society rebuke us
We won't pay heed to them...]

These above lines are taken from well identified *Agomoni Sangeet*, where the mother of Goddesses Uma (Durga) laments about her pain in getting her daughter married. She can only visit her daughter once a year in the month of autumn. That does not suffice her desires of keeping her daughter close to her in her own residence as that would be treated as a disruption from the societal customs. *Agomoni Sangeet* are basically known as "Songs of Advent", a category of Bengali folk songs reveling the arrival of the Goddess Parvati to her home from Kailash, Lord Shiva's abode. These songs refer to the homecoming of Parvati Bengal, not as Deity but as a daughter. The folklore that is prevalent contributes to the basis of these songs. The goddess Durga (Parvati)—is the daughter of the King of the Himalayas. She espouses Lord Shiva who is as the eternal recluse and a pauper. Parvati's mother goddess Menaka dream and longing for her daughter insisted her husband to take along Durga home.

Bengal is well aquainted with the *Agomoni* Songs that welcome goddess Durga prior to the exquisite Durga Puja. This recent paper shall focus into the *Agomoni* Songs; bring out the segregation, the boundaries between the archetypal goddess' parental residence and her husband's abode in Kailash. This further obscure the study by considering the journey of *Maa* Durga from Kailash to her parents and then again back to Kailash (on *Bijaya Dashami*) as movement from one place to another not compelled by her own desire but enforced by social norms, where the Goddesses and her family has to negotiate her constant personal and emotional loss. The word 'Diaspora' comes into play here. Derived from the Greek word *Diaspeiro*, this word carries literal meaning of scattering or dispersion of people from their homeland. While cross-regional and cross-cultural weddings seem to be stirring more often, it is Bengali brides who seem to be traveling to distant and socially strange, sometimes rural destinations away from their own homeland, much similar to the Goddesses. This paper uncovers this bridal diaspora not only through the mythical stories evolving round *Agomoni* but also portraying Ashima the protagonist from Jhumpa Lahiri's *The Namesake*. It finds that in West Bengal, large number of brides has to travel from India to various alien lands under "forced exiles" or 'self-imposed exiles'.... However, travelling as a bride achieves both matrimonial security and work. Sexual and reproductive labours conglomerate with financial labour, directing to the gradually multifaceted forms of journeying in which women are encapsulated.

This paper proposes to discover the character of Ashima who is well-defined as either wife or the mother even though she and her flight of involvements occupy a substantial space in the novel. The theme that has extensively dealt with in the perspective of this novel is the cross-cultural identity crisis. Beginning her life in the close-knitted Kolkata home Ashima graduates from the University of Calcutta in all the rational and psychosomatic magnitudes of English Literature. But no matter how much a girl is provided with a Western education, her life has to be demarcated by the only element of matrimony. She is presented to be the compliant daughter of her parents who unthinkingly slides into a *saree* when asked to by her mother. And this happens out of the blue one day while returning from her college. She tamely stands and sits in front of the parents of Ashok when and as asked to. Her unhesitating respect further ranges up to performing Wordsworth's "Daffodils" as an evidence of what she has acquired so far in her academics of English literature.

Inevitably I feel to compare, Ashima and the mother Goddesses—Uma, both identified as the daughter, the apple of their parents' eyes and then ascertained as obligated wife. In another *Agomoni*, we find this emphasis, from the mother of the Goddesses, that Lord Shiva is insignificant in comparison to Gauri (the other name of the Goddesses) because she has all the qualities to retain herself as the virtuous consort.

Bhangor Bhikhari Jamai Tomar
Sonar Bhromori Gouri Amar

[Pauper is your Son-in-Law
My daughter is one in million]

Ashima—young, vibrant and educated Bengali girl is pretty cautiously presented in the marriage market. The concept of arranged marriage and the marriage market are weaved together here where the matches are made not in heaven on the basis of love but in a market on the basis of fair bargain. Ashima is described as tall and having sharp features—something quite unusual among typical Bengali girls—"Ashima was five feet four inches tall for a Bengali woman" (9). But she possesses those unusual features. Further, being well-versed in the Western language, especially in the literature, which, according to the bourgeoisies Bengali, is a sign of intellectual personality, acts as a supplementary to her credibility in the marriage market. And of course, she can cook and knit well as her mother skillfully places her daughter's expertise in front of the Ashok's family, "She is fond of cooking, and she can knit extremely well. Within a week she finished this cardigan I am wearing" (7). Even Ashima feels amused by the salesmanship of her mother who is determined to keep no stones unturned in front of the boy's family, "Ashima smiled, amused by her mother's salesmanship" (7). With all the mentioned potentials Ashima could have been easily portrayed as the self-dependent headstrong girl who is well aware of her strengths and limitations. Instead, she is framed with the conventional Bengali feminine geography where her character was not provided with the choice of standing on her own feet rather than her husband's.

The conventional notion of women being the nurturer and not the ambitious one is what evidently gets reflected here and also through the portrayal of the goddess Durga. In a way she conveys the typical bourgeois Bengali household who, has to be strikingly appealing in appearance and be a *Dasabhuja* (having ten hands—in accordance to the goddess), fulfilling the domestic chores and skillful in the outer sphere as well.

> *Jaya Jaya He Mahishasura Mardini*
> *Ramya Kapardini Shaila Suthe*
> *Ayi sumana sumana*
> *Sumana sumanohara kanthiyuthe*
> *Sritha rajani rajani rajani*
> *Rajaneekaravakthra vruthe*
> *Sunayana vibhramarabhrama*
> *Bhramarabrahmaradhipadhe*
> *Jaya Jaya He Mahishasura Mardini*
> *Ramya Kapardini Shaila Suthe*
>
> [Salutations to the Divine Mother Whose Beautiful Mind is United with a Charming Appearance. Whose Beautiful Face makes Subserviant the Beauty of the Moon Light of Night by hiding them with Its Beauty. Whose Beautiful Eyes Conquer the Beauty of the Bees by Their Own Beauty. Victory to You, the Destroyer of the Demon Mahishasura, Who has Beautiful Locks of Hair and who is the Daughter of the Mountain.]

The paper studies the distresses of the woman migrating, here Ashima who is at par with the distresses (commonly said as *durgati* in Bengali) of the archetypal mother—Goddess Durga, commonly named as Uma. The paper deals with the mythical annotations related to the displacement and diaspora faced by *Gouri*—the other name of the Goddess and find an analogy with Ashima suffering from bridal diaspora post marriage and her survival strategy. "Ashima has been consuming this concoction throughout her pregnancy, a humble approximation of the snack sold for pennies on Calcutta sidewalks and on railway platforms throughout India, spilling from newspaper cones" (1). On reaching a foreign land with a stranger who is now her husband and hence a little more than a simply known person she is first confronted by the silence of the place. There is no hubbub in here like it used to be back in her Kolkata home. Everything is well-furnished and skillfully showcased. Her first reaction to all of these was confining. I am compelled to compare her distress with the depictions of Neeta, Anasua and Sita by Ritwik Ghatak in his Partition Trilogy identified as distressed images of *Bongomata* (Women of the Golden Land of Bengal). It hints to the *mis*balance between *Prakriti* and *Purush* leading to foreseeable catastrophe. What is noteworthy is that it is not only in *The Namesake* but in all other works of Jhumpa Lahiri feminism is not directly dealt with but it lies right there as an undercurrent wave passing through every layers of the story.

> Though she never explicitly addresses womanism by name in her fiction, the womanistic manifestations of Jhumpa Lahiri in her various works of fiction provide an insightful point of exploration. (Kasun)

The issue of Ashima is addressed not directly but at each and every stage of every character's journey through their experiences. Ashima solitary dependence on Ashok, conforms to the idea of restrained freedom prevalent in Bengali society. Lahiri depicts Ashima, in *The Namesake* as the eldest daughter of the culturally rich family, surviving in a stifling, desperate environment facing the strain of migration. "Ashima thinks it's strange that her child will be born in a place most people enter either to suffer or to die [...]. In India, she thinks to herself, women go home to their parents to give birth, away from husbands and in-laws and household cares, retreating briefly to childhood when the baby arrives" (4). Gender is now largely understood as performance which is constantly shifting. The transformed identity of Lahiri's Ashima from the refined girl to that of the sole homemaker is in itself a journey. The central concern of the women is not limited to negotiating the relationship between the home and the world. Like other migrating women she fights to adapt and acculturate. I specifically compare her with Ritwik Ghatak's Neeta from *Meghe Dhaka Tara* (*The Cloud-Capped Star*) succumbing after being successful in establishing the family; who also portrays the image of the sacrificial mother. Her piercing cry—"*Dada ami kintu banchte cheyechilam, Dada ami banchte boro bhalobasi... Dada ami banchbo...*" [Dada (elder brother) I wanted to live, Dada I would love to live... Dada I would live...]. Perhaps, the muffled voice of Ashima suffering the pain from her water break while giving birth to her first child and not receiving the news of her father's death, journeys through the same loss of *belongingness* in the foreign land. The associated longing for the Goddesses' mother to see Uma, reigns supreme in the *Agomoni Sangeet* as well. It is undeniable that the loss is fervent in the same strain.

Barsa Gelo Aswin Elo
Uma Elo Koi?
Nai Sasuri, Nonod Umar
Ador Korar Nai
Keu Ador Korar Nai
Anadore Kali Mekhe
Berai Pothe Tai

[The rains, Autumn has passed
Uma, why didn't she come?
She has no relatives
To care for her
Nobody to care for her
Loss of care makes her distraught
She now wanders alone]

Ashima's conservation of the varied Bengali rituals in the new land epitomizes the bond with native India. The celebration of Gogol's *Annaprasan* (rice ceremony) as per the Bengali convention provides Ashima an impermanent relief in this foreign atmosphere. On the other hand, to perform this ritual, abscncc of thc family members overshadows Ashima which denotes her longing to create the Bengali atmosphere in the new unknown country. Ashima, Ashoke and Bengali immigrants obey the religious festivals of Christmas and New Year celebration probably to reconcile with the culture. Reversely, the eagerness and excitement of the second-generation Bengali immigrants are observed in celebrating the American festivals than worshiping of Indian Gods and Goddesses.

Ashoke and Ashima, who represent the first-generation immigrants, attempt to hold on to their ethnic and cultural past in an effort to preserve a cultural heritage that is slipping fast in an alien land. "For the sake of Gogol and Sonia they celebrate, with progressively increasing fanfare, the birth of Christ, an event the children look forward to far more than the worship of Durga and Saraswati" (64). Mita Biswas explains how these first-generation immigrants try to cultivate a cultural tradition in their children. These efforts, she observes, touch upon language, religion and literature—

> In order to preserve their culture in the foreign land, the first generation immigrants train their children in the Bengali language, literature and history and expose them to their religious customs, traditions, beliefs, food habits, and social mannerisms. Along with this, they also train them in the ways of the new land and social customs. In the novel, Ashima teaches Gogol to memorize a children's poem by Tagore and the names of deities adorning the ten-handed Durga. (Biswas)

A comparison can be sought between the migrating birds and humans, here Ashima becoming parallel to the large percentage of birds in danger because their habitats or homelands are disappearing. The study of migration or travel-paths of the migrating birds shows that the lack of space for the birds due to increasing human 'development' and consequent loss of ecological conservation are causing mass scale extinction. Space or place determines the movement of time in the novel. The foreign land has not only a power to change the course of the Ashima's life, to shape and reshape her identity, but has also the power to shape time. However, there is a deeper force at work—the character of Ashima is strongly sensitive to the spatial-temporal dimensions of the foreign land and its landscape, culture, and histories. The sense of "non-places" can be located in the migrating lives, their fears and their longing for a piece of land in the foreign land. Ashima physically inhabits these 'non-places.' For her these 'non-places' are marked by an intense perception of her displacement in both time and place and in a perpetual fear of movement through time and place. For her, place is a 'moment' of a gratification of desire—a desire to own a piece of land in the geographical 'place' as well as a desire for an 'acknowledgement' of her presence in the everyday flow of time and life. A famous *Bisorjon Geet* (songs sung during/after the immersion of the idols), substantiates the loss and the separation of Uma, the mother goddess from her mother Menoka apposite to the trauma of Ashima.

> *Jao Go Uma tomar Ghor*
> *Sunyo Kore Mor Ghor*
> *Dukhini Ma Roibo Kemone*
> *Tomai Bidai Diya Go*
> *Ai Go Uma Kole Elo...*
>
> [Return Uma—the place you call home
> My home is now vacant
> I am the distraught mother
> How to stay without you...]

This paper tries to capture the identity (re)formation and resolution of Ashima who resettled in the alien country with her husband. The study also initiates the relation between identity of the migrants and the acculturation process. The aims of this study are twofold. First, its goal is to contribute to the existing literature on theories of identity formation by examining identity distress, crisis, and resolution experienced by a group of refugees after resettlement. "Somehow, this small miracle causes Ashima to feel connected to Cambridge in a way she has not previously thought possible" (42). Second, this study endeavors to explore the effects of identity issues on acculturation strategies. According to many scholars, newcomers generally choose one of four acculturation strategies: separation, marginalization, assimilation, or integration. Integration enables Ashima to achieve a synthesis between the culture of origin and the new host culture. This strategy has been associated with adaptive adjustment results. "Having been deprived of the company of her own parents upon moving to America, her children's independence, their need to keep their distance from her, is something she will never understand" (117). In this vein, this paper examines the acculturation attitudes of West Bengal migrants and the effects of identity issues on variations in acculturation attitudes. Since identity issues are likely to influence acculturation and psychological well-being of resettling groups, this study argues that greater attention needs to be directed at the intersection of immigrant settlement, acculturation, and identity development.

Durga the goddess symbolizes the divine feminine principle, the source of fertility and power. But from the *Agomoni* song we are able to touch upon the inner resources that she retains to adapt, adjust and protect and also reinvent herself in a strange and hostile environment in Kailash (Lord Shiva's address). Here Giriraj, father of Uma, brings her to Girirani the ever lamenting mother Menoka for five days stay in her parental home in the month of autumn saying that their daughter had turn out to be the nitty-gritty of Lord Shiva:

> *Girirani, Ei Nao Tomar Uma Re*
> *Dhoro Dhoro Hare R Jibondhon*
> *Ei Nao Tomar Umare...*
> *Pran Umare Anilam Nijo Kore*
> *Ei Nao Tomar Umare*
> *O Ranga Choron O Duti*
> *Hride Rakhen Dhurjati*
> *Girirani, Ei Nao Tomar Uma Re*
>
> [The Queen of Mountain, here is your daughter Uma
> She is now the crux of Shiva's life
> Here I bring your daughter to our realm...
> I had to plead, so that Shiva allows
> Now I bring her as my own
> Her smeared feet
> Shiva keeps on his chest
> Here I bring your daughter to our realm]

My paper gives me the scope to see settlement in a new country which might mean a much more secure life in a physical and material sense, but a sense of self-sameness likely to be threatened. The resettlement process can hint a tremendous change and, during the process of adaptation and acculturation, Ashima becomes confused and distressed about the new set of values, norms, and ideals to which she is exposed. Her social and personal identities are likely to be challenged by the new socio-cultural context. Individuals in this situation may try to locate her within both ethnic and host cultures or attempt to retain identification with their ethnic culture. Analysis of acculturation data might hint at diverse orientations regarding customs and values, social relations and leisure activities. Engagements in social relations and leisure activities with the 'new' society clinging to their 'old' ways of life, values and practices can give an interesting scope in Ashima's life. This paper tries to convey Lahiri's observations on Ashima, the immigrant going beyond the conventional wisdom and creates the 'third space' where she creates her identity as transnational. Homi K. Bhabha's in his book *The Location of Culture* gives the concept of 'third space' (third space where we negotiate between different identities) which is reinforced and is the common ground of negotiation and transformation, which is neither assimilation nor otherness but represents the history of coalition building and the transnational and cultural diasporic connection.

Migration and displacement bring about the pivot for the reconsideration of structures that help in the edifice and the re-construction of notions of home and other units like nation and culture. "Ashima feels lonely suddenly, horribly, permanently alone, and briefly, turned away from the mirror, she sobs for her husband. She feels overwhelmed by the thought of the move she is about to make, to the city that was once home and is now in its own way foreign" (278). Thus, we notice the altering charts of private, domestic and ethnic identity. Travel due to immigration had fetched into front a disjointed nation and here Lahiri identifies with Ghatak's narratives and identify us with the yearning and memory—the suffering of enforced migration, separating one's family and a recognized penetrating realm. (All translations in this article are by the present author.)

Works Cited

Anwar, Nadia. *Aestheticism, Postmodernism and Displacement in Jhumpa Lahiri's Fiction: A Novel View of the Search for Fulfillment by Obliviating the Past*. Anchor Academic Publishing, 2015. Print.

Batra, Jagdish. *Jhumpa Lahiri's The Namesake: A Critical Study.* Prestige Books, 2010. Print.

Bhabha, Homi K. *The Location of Culture.* 1st ed., Routledge, 1994. Print.

Biswas, Mita. "Cultural Dilemmas in Jhumpa Lahiri's *The Namesake*" in Gourishankar Jha (ed.) *Women Writers in English: A Comprehensive Study.* New Delhi: Authors Press, 2008. Print.

Brah, Avtar. *Cartographies of Diaspora: Contesting Identities.* 1st ed., Routledge, 1996. Print.

Chakravorty Spivak, Gayatri. *A Critique of Postcolonial Reason.* illustrated ed., Harvard University Press, 1999. Print.

Das, Nigamananda. *Jhumpa Lahiri Critical Perspectives.* Pencraft International, 2008. Print.

Datema, Jessica, and Diane Krumrey (Eds.) *Wretched Refuge: Immigrants and Itinerants in the Postmodern.* 1st ed., Cambridge Scholars Publishing, 2010. Print.

Jain, Jasbir. *Writers of Indian Diaspora: Theory and Practice.* Rawat Publications, 1998. Print.

Joseph, Gladys Francis. *Negotiating Identity: A Study of the Fiction of Jhumpa Lahiri.* Jabatan Inggeris, 2012. Print.

Kasun, Genna Welsh. "Womanism and Fiction of Jhumpa Lahiri." Vermont: The University of Vermont, 2009. Print.

Kumar, Amitava (ed.) *Away: The Indian Writer as an Expatriate.* Routledge, 2011. Print.

Kuortti, Joel, and Jopi Nyman. *Reconstructing Hybridity: Post-Colonial Studies in Transition.* Rodopi, 2007. Print.

Lahiri, Jhumpa. *The Namesake.* Mariner Books, 2004. Print.

Said, Edward W. *The World, The Text and The Critic.* Harvard University Press, 1983. Print.

Samad, Shaikh. *Literature of Diaspora: Cultural Dislocation.* Creative Books, 2009. Print.

Varvogli, Aliki. *Travel and Dislocation in Contemporary American Fiction.* 1st ed., Routledge, 2012. Print.

Warner, William Lloyd and Leo Srole. *The Social Systems of American Ethnic Groups.* Vol. 3, Greenwood Press, 1976. Print.

Being at Home:
(Dis)Locating the Self

5

Exile is Not Home: A Reading of Chinua Achebe's *Home and Exile*

Debaditya Mukhopadhyay

> What His Book *Mister Johnson* Did For Me Though Was To Call Into Question My childhood assumption of the innocence of stories. (Achebe, *Home and Exile*)

Chinua Achebe's thought provoking discourse published in the form of the book *Home and Exile* (2000), might be referred as a discussion on how and why some stories misrepresented Africa and how the Africans reacted to this. Before discussing Achebe's own ideas, it seems justified to begin with a basic question: how deceivingly innocent can the word 'story' be? The etymological note of the word has the following information to offer: "Meaning 'recital of true events' first recorded late 14c.; sense of 'narrative of fictitious events meant to entertain' is from c. 1500. Not differentiated from history until 1500s. As a euphemism for 'a lie' it dates from 1690s" (Etymoline). Looking at the changing shades of meaning of this particular word, one cannot help noting that the word has started moving away from truth itself. The question is why? Is it just a modest desire for painting the narratives with extravagance of imagination that made the stories move further away from remaining simply as recital of true events or something more? Besides, the very proximity between story and history seems problematic. If listening to stories is one of the oldest habits of mankind, then one needs to think what kind of stories mankind grew up listening to? There were stories that were mostly made of what exactly happened and then there were stories that followed the principle Aristotle spoke about in *Poetics* and represented what might have happened.

If one takes a look at what Aristotle said while making a distinction between a poet, an idea about the possible way the very notion of narrating what might have been instead of what was, opened, possibly unknowingly, the portals for involving the politics of representation, might be understood. The word 'poet' should not literally and exclusively refer to a poet in *Poetics* because as explained by Anthony Kenny Aristotle was not precisely talking about poetry in his treatise. Kenny observes: "The Greek word *poiesis* (literally 'making'), as used by Aristotle, has both a narrower and a wider scope than the English word 'poetry'" and added that "The closest modern equivalent to Aristotle's word is the German *Dichtung*, which covers prose fiction as well as verse" (Kenny xi). Therefore, it seems that Aristotle was talking chiefly about writers who use their imagination while narrating probable outcomes of a situation involving particular characters. Looking at another significant passage of *Poetics* it is found that "poetry speaks more of universals, history of particulars. By 'universals' I mean the kinds of thing a certain type of person will probably or necessarily do in a given situation" (*Poetics* 69). Eurocentrism is defined as "The conscious or unconscious process by which Europe and European cultural assumptions are constructed as, or assumed to be, the normal, the natural or the universal" (Ashcroft 91). What Aristotle says about the poets' ability, that is to conceive the universals is indeed an incredible ability and the present discussion does not intend to malign that but if one simply tries to imagine a European writer trying to forge out of his or her mind a detailing of what a non-European might do in a particular situation, one is bound to get reminded of the problem of Eurocentrism. What a European writer starts imagining about the way a certain non-European might behave runs under the risk of getting tinged by the discourses of Eurocentrism and hence the problem with stories told by Europeans about Africa or Arabia or China or India and so on.

Though Edward Said's seminal work *Orientalism* (1978) had already talked about the way narratives about the Orient (both fictional and non-fictional) managed to establish Europeans in a superior position compared to the non-Europeans, Said's significant and cogent voice had not spoken for the Africans.

Salman Rushdie had given the clarion call in 1982 regarding the Empire writing back to the Emperors and the impact of the Rushdie-slogan got intensified as soon as it got deservedly hijacked by Ashcroft, Griffiths, and Tiffin for their pioneering book in 1989. As mentioned in the "Preface", Achebe's lectures were delivered in 1998, a little after the aforementioned significant events. The book, though it borrows Rushdie's slogan significantly for the title of one of the three major sections, seems to offer a few other necessary thoughts that appear to be much needed for understanding the response of the ruled people against the literature of the rulers. Achebe seems to have followed a strategy that is explained in connection with the model of the dominated and dominating one mentioned by Ashcroft, Griffiths, and Tiffins in their book. The trio suggests that by following this model, "the social and literary relations of oppressor and oppressed communities" (Ashcroft, *The Empire Writes Back* 31) may be discussed and "A characteristic of dominated literatures is an inevitable tendency towards subversion". They add that "a study of the subversive strategies employed by post-colonial writers would reveal both the configurations of domination and the imaginative and creative responses to this condition" (Ashcroft, *The Empire Writes Back* 32). This paper will attempt to show how Achebe's arguments in *Home and Exile* depict the impact that the stories by non-Africans had on the Africans especially the young minds.

Achebe begins by recollecting a few of his childhood memories related to his family's return to Ogidi. He belonged to a generation that from their birth saw various facets of the Empire gradually settling down upon the Africans. Achebe very clearly admits that his father had become instrumental in the spreading of Christianity and yet it never seems that Achebe's father had an issue with African people or their culture *per se*. Achebe recollects, "Both my parents were strong and even sometimes uncompromising in their Christian beliefs, but they were not fanatical" (Achebe 10). In the beginning section of the book Achebe narrates how his homecoming had not turned out to be pleasant initially. The Ogidi people identified Achebe's family as that of a man associated with a foreign religion but gradually the veranda of their house, the piazza started having meetings between the non-Christians and Achebe's Christian family. Achebe writes, "Our home was open to them all, and my father received his peers and relatives—Christian or not—with kola nut and palm-wine in that piazza" (Achebe 11). How actually this family reacted to their heathen friends and relatives become clear looking at the incident between Achebe's father and his half-brother. This half-brother had taken the opportunity of placing a heathen shrine in his Christian half-brother's house in his absence. Achebe's father did protest against this, but at the same time Achebe felt that his father actually found this to be ironical.

The narrative at this point tries also to give readers an idea about how peculiar the Ogidi people must have felt about the gradual settling down of Christian religion amongst them. First, these people were totally unwilling to impose their own religion upon anyone else, which Achebe shows by referring to how Ogidi people willingly gave a group of migrants amongst them two of their Ogidi-gods but only after renaming them in a manner that allowed the migrants to get gods that represented the successors of the Ogidi-gods that the migrants were interested in. Secondly, Ogidi people were believers in individuality, which again is illustrated in the book by referring to the story that shows Chukwu, the Creator making arrangements for separate and individual residence of the first ancestors of two different communities. Achebe comments, "As I learned more and more about Igbo people, it began to dawn on me that this insistence on separate and individual creations of towns chimed perfectly with the belief that every single human being was a unique creation of chi" (Achebe 15-16). All these interesting folklores used by Achebe explains how important the concept of home was for the Ogidi people or for that matter every African whose minds were nourished by not exactly same but equivalent folklores that must have taught them to know the value of their home that is, the place that allows them to remain as individuals and respect the fact that others too have their own houses which they call home. Achebe himself seems to have made an apt equation in the book, a sense about the value of individuality alias home was developed for ages in Ogidi minds by their traditional folklores and creation myths which it seems to have been considered by Achebe as bricks that built the metaphorical 'Home' and then came the imperial forces of Europeans that set fire on these long nurtured homes.

Why the birth of African literature seemed extremely important in this situation is explained when Achebe says: "Those hundreds of autonomous Igbo villages and towns, so deeply suspicious of political amalgamation, would be stretched to the limit should they ever face an enemy able to wield the resources of a centralized military power, acting directly or through local surrogates. They would need every fortification to be found in their histories and creation myths" (Achebe 17). In the quoted portion he seems to point out how unprecedented appeared the cohesive force used by the imperialists for the people under attack and hence the attacked, for finding a solution had to get back to their metaphorical homes, built through the ages by adding one folklore and mythical tale upon another. This certainly necessitated the birth of African literature, but parturition comes with inevitable moments of pain and struggle, the next portion of Achebe's monograph takes note of that. James Currey's words seem to aptly capture African literature's comparatively delayed arrival amidst other literatures whose writers were not British and who tended to use English language for a special reason:

> English was the lubricant of the English-speaking world. It was not only how authority was imposed but it was also the way in which the subject peoples reacted to that imposition of power. Writers in India, the Caribbean and Africa came to take advantage of the language that they shared, but they had to have publishing opportunities. And to begin with those opportunities were almost all in London. By 1962 quite a lot of work by Caribbean writers had been published in London. Some Indian writers were well-established on London lists. But practically no creative work by Africans had appeared. (Achebe 1-2)

Along with this issue, Achebe identified a few others. He identified how the situation was made even more problematic was the fact that in the absence of African writers' own writings, there prevailed English texts that spoke about Africa and was written by non-Africans which were not only read but taught academically. He made it clear that he was not uncomfortable with English literature as a whole. Rather, he admits to be an admirer of *Gulliver's Travels*, *Ivanhoe*, etc. He says: "I was entranced by the faraway and long-ago worlds of the stories, so different from the stories of my home and childhood" (Achebe 21). Not the same could be said by him about works like *Mister Johnson* by Joyce Cary which he had to read as a student. Though this novel was highlighted by Achebe's teachers as an excellent portrayal of Africa, the whole class ended up disagreeing with that. Achebe, speaking about his personal reaction says that he did not have a specific issue with the fact that the Nigerian hero is shot to death by a British in the novel, but what he found problematic was the way "at the slightest chance, a contagion of distaste, hatred and mockery breaks through to poison" Cary's novel. His ultimate realization about the issue with Cary's text is:

> In the end I began to understand. There is such a thing as absolute power over narrative. Those who secure this privilege for themselves can arrange stories about others pretty much where, and as, they like. Just as in corrupt, totalitarian regimes, those who exercise power over others do anything. They can bring out crowds of demonstrators whenever they need them. (Achebe 24-25)

In the discussion Achebe not only makes the reader aware of the thriving tradition of writings about Africa but also makes the important observation: "A tradition does not begin and thrive, as the tradition of British writing about Africa did, unless it serves a certain need" (Achebe 28). By referring to a critical study on literature regarding Africa by Dorothy Hammond and Alta Jablow, Achebe argues that such writings at first had become an auxiliary support for the Slave trade but eventually by the time when the Slave trade itself ended, this tradition had "also generated a life of its own" and began to have newer and possibly more insidious purposes. At first it was only Joyce Cary's book that caught Achebe's attention but eventually he began to understand that even the Rider Haggard or John Buchan books that he read in childhood had the same problem. With this awareness Achebe began to consciously detect to what extent such books as mentioned above attacked his metaphorical home. He writes:

> What *Mister Johnson* did do for me was not to change my course in life and turn me from something else into a writer.... But it did open my eyes to the fact that my home was under attack and that my home was not merely a house or a town but, more importantly, an awakening story in whose ambience my own existence had first begun to assemble its fragments into a coherence and meaning. (Achebe 38)

What Achebe might have ended up doing after this point was the unleashing of a vehement attack on British writers but like a wise and mature critic and writer he is, he refrains from doing so and instead mentions the significant difference he found in the book *West Africa* by F.J. Pedler. He says: "What I find truly remarkable about Pedler's book is the prominence he gave to and the faith he had in, African literature that was not even in existence yet" (Achebe 42). Pedler, despite being a non-African had written emphatically about the need for West-Africans to pick up the pen and give the world authentic stories about themselves and Achebe, along with a few other significant authors began doing precisely that. Achebe provides a list featuring more than five significant works that arrived in a row during the 1950s. He does not homogenize all these works simply as the Empire responding to its centre but points out: "The new literature that erupted...in the 1950s and 1960s showed great variety in subject matter, in style of presentation.... But there was one common thread...the thread of a shared humanity linking the author to the world of his creation" (Achebe 49). Such an observation indeed sheds light on a very important aspect of these works. It was not that these writers were blindly in love with the world that they were writing about but they made it clear that the world they chose to write about was the very same they themselves belonged to.

After this point Achebe's work moves into a discussion that is equally interesting. If the Home was under attack and attempts of defending those attacks began from the 1950s, there remains still the question of what happened in Exile about this defending of the Home. Achebe traces such repercussions pointing out how reviewers did a complete bashing of this newly emergent literature. The case of Elspeth Huxley is used very significantly in this context. Despite the fact that this woman writer of considerable merit had a direct experience of African life she found only malignant elements in *The Palm-Wine Drinkard*. If this was the reaction of a woman basically belonging to the world outside Africa, Achebe does not forget to mention that there were also some striking negative reviews from Nigerian students or Buchi Emecheta regarding this novel of Tutuola or works following a similar ideology. His conclusion about such a reaction is the reverberating line: "The psychology of the dispossessed can be truly frightening" (Achebe 72). Achebe, being a witness of the Empire beginning to write back seems also aware of the possible repercussions such efforts of writing back is likely to initiate. The discourses that prevailed before have already created an acute loss of self-esteem in Africans and besides he acknowledges the fact that even this act of writing back might just get reduced to being a fashionable act and a mushroom growth of copycats might just follow. He also clarifies that this writing back will not certainly be purely a counter-attack on Europeans reversing the mechanism of demonization, but he reminds that "in the final reckoning the universal conversation will be not copycats but those able to bring hitherto untold stories, along with new ways of telling" (Achebe 83).

In the last section of his work Achebe seems a little judgemental of writers like V.S. Naipaul who "ask everybody to shut down their history, pack their bag and buy a one-way ticket to Europe or America" (Achebe 91). He tries to explain in this section that the trend of Artists moving into exile that remarkably began during the Modernist era might not be a good option for artists from the poorer section of the world. The option of exile might just look tempting and filled with hopes of finding a better world but it is not so. He clarifies that he is, however, not trying to be a dictator and decide for every writer writing back where they should belong to. He clarifies,

"I am concerned only with the advertisement of expatriation and exile as intrinsically desirable goals for the writer or as the answer to the problem of unequal development in the world" (Achebe 96). He sounds very practical when he says analyzing a significant novel: "The young African, Samba Diallo, will, however, discover that, contrary to the optimistic notions of his people, Europe has made no real provision for his participation" (Achebe 98). What Achebe says seems to highlight an insidious aspect of Neo-colonialism. By consistently depicting the once colonized world to be inferior in comparison with the First World, a willful migration towards the First World is getting initiated. Africans are again moving to the areas the First World always wanted them to move towards, only for an apparently different reason. Hence, Achebe's work does not simply turn out to be just another cry to join the chorus of Empire writing back, but it reminds that writing back means not simply fighting back. It means to begin a conversation and though he gives Rushdie due credits for pointing this out, he does not refrain from commenting that Rushdie's notion of Literature having very little to do with a writer's home address is at the best one that will restrict the writer's ability to explore all the hidden nooks of his Home.

Works Cited

Achebe, Chinua. *Home and Exile.* New York: Anchor Books, 2000. Print.

Ashcroft, Bill, Gareth Griffiths and Helen Tiffin. *Post-Colonial Studies: The Key Concepts.* New York: Routledge, 2009. Print.

———. *The Empire Writes Back.* 2nd Edition. New York: Routledge, 2002. Print.

Currey, James. "Introduction." Currey, James. *Africa Writes Back.* Ohio: Ohio University Press, 2008. 1-36. Print.

Etymonline. 3 March 2018 <https://www.etymonline.com/word/story>. Web.

Kenny, Anthony. "Introduction." *Poetics.* London: Oxford University Press, n.d. vii-xxxviii. Print.

"Poetics." *Classical Literary Criticism.* Trans. Penelope and T.S. Dorsch Murray. London: Penguin, 2004. 57-97. Print.

6

Displacement and Madness: Situating (Mad) Woman Outside the Attic

Samata Biswas

> ...I often wonder who I am and where is my country and where do I belong....

Do all women end up in the attic?

While reading *Wide Sargasso Sea*, the thought constantly haunted me...does the world become the *attic* when women do not fit in the given stereotypical category of 'Woman'? When some women try to look at the world with a different gaze, the gaze that is not the 'conquering gaze from nowhere', rather a gaze more situated, located on her own experience and knowledge does they find themselves inside the *attic* of insanity, unreason? As epitomized in Antoinette's statement to Rochester in the above-mentioned quotation (Rhys 77), the question of socio-psychological location becomes pertinent the moment stereotypes are broken.

In *Wide Sargasso Sea*, Antoinette Cosway is portrayed as a free spirited, rebellious woman who does not fit into the typical frame of English Woman. Her childhood is spent in Coulibri, Jamaica. Her father was a slave owner. But after the abolition of slavery her family lost their fortune. After her father's death, because of poverty Antoinette's mother, Annette remarried wealthy Englishman Mr. Mason. The freed slaves out of their suppressed anger burned their house when they saw their recovering prosperity; the fire affected their lives more by killing Antoinette's mentally disabled younger brother. Antoinette's mother's mental health was always unsettling, but losing her son pushed her to the verge of insanity. Her mother was sent to live with a couple where she was tortured and later, she died. Antoinette's childhood was full of trauma as she never felt as she belonged to the 'white skinned' community, neither she was accepted among the coloured skin people. Her mother's 'madness' haunted her throughout her life. Even after her marriage her husband (Rochester, although this name was never used in the book) believed that madness is in her blood, which drove her more toward drunkenness and insanity. Antoinette, renamed by her husband as Bertha, was moved to England to the Thornfield Hall, the Rochester mansion. She is confined to 'the attic'. She only has a relationship with Grace, the servant who is appointed to guard her. Mr. Rochester hides her from the world. He eventually stops visiting her. He pursues relationships with other women and later he decides to marry the governess, Jane Eyre. At the end, Antoinette dreams of flames surrounds the house, she feels free from the life she has there; waking from her dream she escapes her room, sets the fire and ends her life.

As Rhys builds up Antoinette's character, she creates a 'madness' which is her increased sense of paranoia and her disappointment in her marriage. As *Wide Sargasso Sea* is considered to be the prequel of Jane Eyre (although written by a different author), Antoinette, who is suffering and ends up alone and raving in the attic of Thornfield Hall, becomes the pre-figuration of the madwoman in the attic. She remains hidden from the world.

Throughout the book, while Antoinette represents an ambivalent hybrid, that is, she is neither black nor white, but somewhere in-between Europe and the Caribbean, her husband Edward is an Englishman without the complexity of a mixed background. For Edward, Antoinette seems to be an enigma; she is not white, but not black either, therefore she must be mad. Edward's failure to understand Antoinette is coming from his "white masculine western reason" (Biswas and Dhar 208). In the next section let us explore the dualism of reason-unreason and try to look into madness which may be produced from displacement from reality (Hegel).

Madness: Reason vs. Unreason

> ...madness, in its wild, untamable words, proclaims its own meaning; in its chimeras[1], it utters its secret truth.... (Foucault 30)

What is madness? How do we perceive madness? Many notions of madness have been developed in Philosophy, Psychology, Psychoanalysis as well as in Medicine. There is a science of madness created through time. But with all these notions of madness, do we actually understand it or still is it an enigma? What is the Science of knowing madness? Whose science? Is it Western Science that defines madness? Is it male reason of knowing woman's madness? Is non-reason then reduced to madness?

Defining 'Madness' is problematic. It can be interpreted in various ways. Madness can be viewed as an imbalance in neurotransmitter, a social phenomenon or even a person's cultural differences in practicing norms can be considered as madness. Madness can also be a consequence of oppression in society, such as patriarchal oppression (Tennholt).

Madness has its own truth. That is difficult to unfold with the white masculine western reason (Biswas and Dhar). Whatever we do not understand has to be either not 'normal' or we try to put them under the criteria which relieves us from the discomfort of not understanding. For example, when we do not understand madness, then we come up with notions such as madness runs in the family or one is psychologically too weak to handle pressure; all these indications formulate an easy way out from the responsibility of the society. When the discussion is about 'mad woman', women are considered to have underdeveloped morality (Kohlberg), lack of rationality, etc. Many researches done by psychologists with the androcentric framework creates and reinforces an understanding where women are considered to be emotional. The emotionality (as if) renders them weaker so as to make them incapable of proper logical thinking and even decision-making.

> Those images reinforce the (false) dichotomy of rationality versus emotionality, where emotions are culturally

> defined as that which is not rational, or irrational. That opposition and the resulting images thereby support the apparent neutrality of the "rational man" who retains unquestionable legitimacy when he stands implicitly in opposition to the emotional, irrational, or "hysterical woman" (Calas and Smircich 1993). Such gendered images appear throughout the dominant institutional discourses of Western culture and serve to devalue emotions and reproduce a cultural mandate of emotional control. (Meyerson 107)

With this creation of culturally prescribed characteristics of women she falls under the process of individualization within psychologization which indicates women as the weaker one reflecting the idea that it is all in her mind; which is aided by psychology by creating a different language altogether for them.

In *Wide Sargasso Sea*, Antoinette's 'madness' is a social phenomenon; her husband's behaviour might have driven her 'mad'; also, his patriarchal upbringing could be derived from his role as a colonizer. Mr. Rochester's white supremacy over Antoinette's Creole heritage and her sex make her doubly oppressed. When Antoinette tries to share her knowledge about West Indies, to maintain his superiority and not to show weakness and inferiority, he avoids to be tutored by a woman, by his wife. Rather, he tries to teach Antoinette about England.

Not only he strips her from her property, with showing constant disrespect and dislike for West Indies, he strips her of everything she could earlier claim as her own, of her identity and her being. "I loved this place and you have made it into a place I hate. I used to think that if everything else went out of my life I would still have this, and now you have spoilt it" (Rhys 121). By losing her everything, she also lost her 'sanity'.

Later to his advantage, Antoinette's 'madness' helps him to control her which he carries on by moving her to England, where he confined her not only physically but also mentally.

From Home to Attic and Attic to Home Again

> She said she loved this place. This is the last she'll see of it. I'll watch for one tear, one human tear. Not that blank

> hating moonstruck face. I'll listen.... If she says good-bye perhaps adieu. ...If she too says it, or weeps, I'll take her in my arms, my lunatic. She's mad but mine, mine. ... My lunatic. My mad girl. Here's a cloudy day to help you. No brazen sun. No sun... No sun. The weather's changed. (Rhys 136)

Mr. Rochester abolished Antoinette identity in order to turn her into an English Victorian wife, whom he can control. While leaving for England, he saw she does not express any feelings at all anymore. She has lost her energy and acts completely passively. She was being displaced. Her displacement was not only geographical but also psychological. She lost her home.

Home in a broader sense goes beyond its spatial boundaries. Home is a fluid concept that needs to be constantly 'negotiated.'[2] Home can be one's homeland, a body, a cyberspace, a community, or a place where caring occurs (Schissel). Homelessness can also be due to 'madness'.

Spatial boundaries can also give a sense of confinement. When Antoinette was moved to England, she was in a house but was locked up attic. She did not have the liberty to move around the house. Only with no one's knowledge or in her dreams she roamed around like a ghost. Her sense of freedom was taken away from her. The free spirited Antoinette lost her sense of space and time.

> They tell me I am in England but I don't believe them. We lost our way to England. When? Where? I don't remember, but we lost it. ...this cardboard house where I walk at night is not England. (Rhys 148)

She could not remember or understand where she was and how long she was kept in the attic. She was forced to leave the place she called home, a place where she belonged. He refused to let her lead an independent life by leaving him, he feared losing his patriarchal power and dominance over his wife.

The subjectivities of displaced women are in consideration with the intersectional oppressions of patriarchy, colonialism, etc. Thus the historical experience of difference is based on some socially constructed categories such as race, class, gender, sexuality, or religious, ethnic, or cultural affiliation. Displaces person is the one who has to leave his home (country) may be due to war, etc. In this novel, the forceful displacement was due to the patriarchal and colonizing mind set of Antoinette's husband.

Displacement can be psychological, a defense mechanism, like redirection of an emotion or impulse from its original object (such as an idea or person) to another. Antoinette emotional expressions are at the end displaced; her stream of consciousness was taking her to her 'home', to her childhood.

> Then I turned round and saw the sky. It was red and all my life was in it. I saw the grandfather clock and Aunt Cora's patchwork, all colours, I saw the orchids and the stephanotis and the jasmine and the tree of life in flames. I saw the chandelier and the red carpet downstairs and the bamboos and the tree ferns, the gold ferns and the silver, and the soft green velvet of the moss on the garden wall. I saw my doll's house and the books and the picture of the Miller's Daughter. I heard the parrot call as he did when he saw a stranger, Qui est lá? Qui est là? (Rhys 155)

In Conclusion

Bronte's portrayal of Bertha Mason (aka Antoinette) was of a ghost, who had no agency of her own; any history or a story to tell. She was pitied. Mr. Rochester, on the other hand, was portrayed as a good man who did not send her 'mad' wife to an asylum to rot. He loved his wife but seemed helpless in the face of her madness. Although, he did hide her from the world and made her the 'ghost in the attic'.

During 1890s, there was a trend in Victorian literature to write about women's issues, such as education, marriage, sexuality, motherhood, etc. A new type of woman emerged in literature who not only did not follow but also rejected the given stereotypical roles. H.E.M. Stutfield (Tierny 991-93) divided these novelists into two schools, 'purity school' and 'neurotic school'. The purity school was more inclined toward the nature of the woman who believed in free love and going against the rules given by the society. In most of the cases they were happy and they led their lives differently from the stereotypical structure (to some extent as Jane Eyre was described in Bronte's novel). But in the description of the 'neurotic school', women portrayed as rebels, more cynical, and in most of the novels ended with women facing the consequences of the stigma of having mental illness or had to commit suicide from the pressure resulting from denying the stereotypical roles. *Wide Sargasso Sea* in some ways portrays the 'mad' woman whose subjectivity was moulded by her experience of colonization, patriarchy and her cultural affiliation.

Rhys makes a postcolonial argument by portraying Antoinette's character as trapped between two worlds—Western colonial and Afro-Caribbean. The novel is also considered a feminist work, as it deals with unequal power between men and women, particularly in marriage. May be committing suicide was her escape from patriarchal domination.

Notes

1. An illusion or fabrication of the mind (https://www.merriam-webster.com/dictionary/chimera)
2. Schissel, Wendy. *Home/Bodies: Geographies of Self, Place, and Space*. Calgary, Canada: University of Calgary Press, 2006.

Works Cited

Berthold-Bond, Daniel. *Hegel's Theory of Madness*. SUNY Press, 1995. Print.

Biswas, Ranjita and Anup Dhar. "Rights of the 'Mad' in Mental Health Science" in *Applied Ethics and Human Rights: Conceptual Analysis and Contextual Applications*, Ed. Shashi Motilal. Anthem Press, 2011. Print.

Foucault, Michel. *Madness and Civilization: A History of Insanity in the Age of Reason*. Vintage, 1988. Print.

Hirsch, Marianne. "Pictures of a Displaced Girlhood". In Bammer, Angelika (Ed). *Displacements: Cultural Identities in Question*. Indiana University Press, 1994. Print.

Meyerson, Debra E. "Feeling Stressed and Burned Out: A Feminist Reading and Re-Visioning of Stress-Based Emotions within Medicine and Organization Science", *Organization Science*, Vol. 9, No. 1 (Jan.-Feb.), 1998: 108. Print.

Rhys, Jean. *Wide Sargasso Sea*. New Delhi: Penguin Books, 2000. Print.

Schissel, Wendy. *Home/Bodies: Geographies of Self, Place, and Space*. Calgary, Canada: University of Calgary Press, 2006. Print.

Tennholt, Karolina. "Patriarchal Madness—Patriarchal Oppression and Madness in Jean Rhys's *Wide Sargasso Sea*", Södertörn University College, English Department Fall 2005. http://www.diva-portal.org/smash/get/diva2:16322/fulltext01. Web.

Tierney, Helen. (Ed). *Women's Studies Encyclopedia*. Vol. 2. New Delhi: Rawat Publications, 1999. Print.

7

The Eternal Quest: Home and the Homeless in Amitav Ghosh's *The Hungry Tide*

Zenith Roy

Introduction

> Home is the place where, when you have to go there,
> They have to take you in.[1] (Frost, "Hired Man" 43)

Robert Frost's unconventional, if uncharitable, definition of 'home' stresses upon the 'taking in', i.e. the sense of inclusion and belonging. It is this concept of inclusion and belonging that we name as 'home'. More than a brick-and-mortar construct, the 'home' is a concept that consists of a sense of a relief through the conjuration of the magical image of a soothing haven with heart-warming confines, a cozy and ineffable ambience of gratifying familiarity that lets us be ourselves, feeling safely shielded from the toxic negativities of the world outside. Home is the fountainhead of our existence, a place to which we naturally belong and is thus the embodiment of one of the most powerful yearnings that define the human experience. It is a kind of umbilical bond that consistently keeps the mind fervently longing for the home or the homeland, paining it with an excruciatingly acute yearning to return to that home or the region where it exists or even used to exist.

The Hungry Tide, an expression of the contraries of the happiness of gaining a home and the pain of losing it, is a movingly human saga of deep realisations and devastating experiences as well as a realistic contemplation on the human condition. This paper is an endeavour at figuring out the multiple angles from which Ghosh looks at the question of having and not having a home and endows novel dimensions to the issue with his sensitive approach.

The Hungry Tide: Epicentred in the 'Tide Country'

The setting or the locale is of immense importance in Amitav Ghosh's fiction. To quote the author himself:

> A novel...must always be set somewhere: it must have its setting, and within the evolution of the narrative this setting must clearly play a part almost as important as those of the characters themselves. Location is thus intrinsic to a novel. (*Imam* 296)

However, although 'locatedness' is one of the prime traits of Ghosh's novels, it is a fascinatingly fluid locatedness which effortlessly adapts itself to the spatially and socio-culturally displaced characters and their dislocated existences. Thus Ghosh's fiction, concurrent with its Indian focus, surpasses the same through its intensive involvement with the present-day world of immigrants, refugees and the Ibis trilogy, Ghosh's novels are deeply concerned with their respective settings or rather the flexibility of settings. Ghosh's perpetual penchant for crossing borders and his ironic elimination of the same is amply manifest in his fiction which is his response to the concern of the anthropologist inside him, regarding the porosity of cultural boundaries.

This porosity of the setting gets perfect reflection in *The Hungry Tide* which is located in the Sundarbans, a strange land without borders to isolate the fresh water from the brine or even land from water. The tides, often violent, can reach more than two hundred miles into the land, while thousands of acres of mangrove forests disappear only to re-appear within hours. "This is a land half-submerged at high tide: it is only in *falling* that the water gives birth to the forest. To look upon this strange parturition, midwived by the moon, is to know why the name 'tide country' is not just right but necessary" (*Hungry* 8).

Down the centuries, the land has been the sanctuary of the genuinely dispossessed and the ineffectual dreamers who have dared to settle amidst its tiger, snake and crocodile-infested terrains, barely making a living out of its stubborn soil. The 'tide country' is a borderless entity, a land shorn of certainty and coloured in gray, "a terrain where the boundaries between land and water are always mutating, always unpredictable" (*Hungry* 7). It is a 'utopia', seemingly a nonexistent locale inhabited by people of shifting identities—a place where "it was impossible to tell who was who, and what their castes and religions and beliefs were" (*Hungry* 79).

In the midst of these tricky and treacherous terrains, Ghosh spawns a fictional place, Lusibari, a two-kilometre-long island in the southern end of the Sundarbans, literally insular with no other island in its fifty-kilometre radius. By dint of his deep acquaintance with humanity and his anthropological acumen, Ghosh shapes Lusibari into the utterly credible core of the novel's actions, the assemblage of all its major personages along with their inner intricacies, the emotional ties they share, and the turmoil that complicates their mutual relationships.

A Quest for Home

Despite the relocation of the self and the nation, the characters in Ghosh's fiction evince the typically humane longing for the homeland, a passionate craving that characterizes and, at the same time, problematizes the existential experience of any diaspora across the world. In fact, this yearning for the home or one's native land is the trait that lends a distinctive identity to diasporas which, as defined by Robin Cohen, are "communities shaped by histories of dispersion and immigration between or within continents but for whom an attachment to the homeland, real and imagined, continues to provide a key site of identification, a compelling font of memory" (quoted in Mullaney 7). The sense of the home is inseparably integrated with the sense of the diasporic identity.

People may be physically isolated from their nation, their natural homeland, but the agonizing awareness of that isolation keeps haunting them perpetually like an unrelenting spectre. The quest of improved living standards and better amenities may take people from one point across the globe to another, but they can never isolate themselves from the awareness of their roots, their culture, and their history, things that are too deeply embedded in the human psyche. Torn between the actual homeland and the new settlement, the existential crisis faced by the diasporas deepens, compelling them to create what Salman Rushdie calls 'imaginary homelands' (Rushdie 10).

Ghosh, in his writings, gives a sentient expression to the crisis and trauma suffered by the members of a diasporic community. One of the prime complexities a member of the diaspora faces on coming to their motherland for the first time is the problem of identification, the inability to instantly gel with the people. At the beginning of *The Hungry Tide*, we witness through Kanai's eyes the too obvious foreignness of Piya, the cetologist fresh from the States. "[A]gainst the sooty background of the commuter station at Dhakuria, the neatly composed androgyny of her appearance seemed out of place, almost exotic" (*Hungry* 3-4). However, it is an irony that Kanai himself, despite being purely Indian by birth and citizenship, is also strangely an outsider to the 'tide country'.

Both Piya and Kanai represent the chic, urbane and upper middle-class Bengali driven by the globalized outlook. One of the remarkable aspects of their respective cultural identities is their relationship with language. Piya, with her adherence to the foreign tongue, represents the subversion of Indian languages, while Kanai's existence thrives on the commodification of the languages of this country. But within the peripheries of the tide country they find themselves "adrift on a tide of shifting tongues" (Dattaray 151). Warmth and affection that one experiences in the company of their near ones has always eluded Piya, who has been a helpless member of a dysfunctional family helmed by her ever-warring parents. Although Piya never explicitly says so, we seem to sense a subliminal urgency in her, probably the desperate urge to break away from the suffocating peripheries of a chaotic home. Her return to Lusibari at the end of the novel is nothing but her return to homely warmth and security amongst a people in whom she has found the geniality and affection she has always been hungering for.

On the other hand, Kanai, who is settled in Delhi and oversees an office of translators there, is a denizen of a translated world which is both specious and emotionally void. He is on his first-ever return to the tide country since spending a few months there in 1970 when he was a schoolboy sent to live with his uncle Nirmal and aunt Nilima to be 'rusticated' and made fit for schoolwork. Accustomed with that vacuous urban existence, Kanai is visibly ill at ease while negotiating his journey to the hinterlands. For Kanai, Nilima is his only relation alive and thus Lusibari, where she lives, through the love and affection of his deceased uncle who has left behind his personal testament for Kanai's eyes only, is home in the true sense for him. Hence, the note of hope regarding Kanai's return to Lusibari sounded at the end of the novel makes us look forward to it as a return to his roots, to an address where he actually 'belongs'.

Morichjhāpi: A Dream of a Home Shattered

If the central narrative of *The Hungry Tide* concerns the homecoming of Piya and Kanai in the modern-day world, the foundation of the main storyline is a journey back in history to the shameful incident of human brutality that had occurred in Morichjhāpi.[2]

The Morichjhāpi episode occupies a space of vital importance in the narrative of *The Hungry Tide*, underlining the importance of home and proving how homelessness can compel people to take desperate measures which, in turn, may cause disastrous consequences. A home is never merely an assortment of brick and mortar, but a feeling and a sensation, a sense of security. The Morichjhāpi settlers were desperate, as a result of months and years of uncertainty, hunger and lack of resources to find security, the meagre luxury they sought was a roof above their homeless heads.

The atrocity unleashed upon the Morichjhāpi settlers by the state administration was a starkly painful contrast to the philanthropic ideals of Sir Daniel Hamilton, the individual who had dreamt of establishing a country of sorts across the wide and wild expanse of the tide country, turning it into a utopian landscape with equal opportunity for all to have a home. Kanai recalls Nirmal's account of Sir Hamilton's vision of "a new society, a new kind of country" (*Hungry* 55):

> [I]t was a dream.... He wanted to build a place where on one would exploit anyone and people would live together without petty social distinctions and differences. He dreamed of a place where men and women could be farmers in the morning, poets in the afternoon and carpenters in the evening. (*Hungry* 56)

Faintly resembling Gonzalo's idea of the idyllic commonwealth in *The Tempest* (II, i) in the vision of a society free from discrimination, Sir Hamilton's concept, though it never reached fruition, was something in stark contradiction to the ruthlessly repressive measures undertaken by the state administration to make the settlers evacuate Morichjhāpi. In hindsight, it appears to be a cruel irony that the tide country which was conceived as a home to people of all hue, not only spurned but mauled homeless people who had flocked to it prompted by a dire need of a refuge.

By raking up the almost-forgotten episode of Morichjhāpi, Ghosh moulds his novel into a humanist critique of dispossession in the postcolonial world. The spectral recollections of Morichjhāpi are a shocking pointer to the inadequacy of the postcolonial state to provide a safe 'home' to the marginalized. Thus, Ghosh skilfully juxtaposes the insecurity of homelessness with the reassuring presence of the home, the sense of belonging with that of non-belonging which dogs the refugees who had gathered in the tide-troubled archipelago of the Sundarbans, poignantly articulated in Rilke's lines, as written by Nirmal in his memoir addressed to Kanai:

> Each slow turn of the world carries such disinherited ones to whom neither the past nor the future belong. (*Hungry* 175)

Through the portrayal of the Morichjhāpi settlers, who were mostly of the *namasudra* caste, Ghosh voices the tragedy of the subaltern in *The Hungry Tide*. The torture and inhumanity unleashed upon the Morichjhāpi settlers just adds another appalling chapter to the long history of brutality that subalterns and people belonging to the margins have all along been subjected to in this country by the dominant sections of the society and the powers that be.

This apart, the Morichjhāpi episode exemplifies Ghosh's fascination for going back in history to the past and the background of a place to understand it completely. To quote Ghosh:

> I find history completely absorbing and fascinating. I am always interested to discover aspects of history; it adds a kind of richness to one's experience of place. (Ferdous)

Ghosh's interaction with history vis-à-vis *The Hungry Tide* takes him back to one of the unsavoury episodes of the past and also allows him to juxtapose the binary opposites of the trauma of losing a home with the ecstasy of finding a new one. In respect to this, the question that arises is whether Ghosh intends to present Piya's and Kanai's finding a new home as poetic justice avenging the inhumanity with which the Morichjhāpi settlers were deprived of the home they had dreamt of establishing on the island. One other thing to be noted is the similarity between the circumstances of the destitute population which had gathered on the island and those of Piya's. The bestial living conditions in Dandakaranya had made the refugees stationed there desperate enough to escape and gather in Morichjhāpi. Similarly, Piya, disgusted with living in a suffocating prison of a home afflicted by the ceaseless wrangling between her parents, arrives in the 'tide country', though purportedly for a different reason.

Piya's Journey: An Inward Odyssey that Comes a Full Circle

The journey embarked upon by Piya from America to the tide country, though purportedly an extension of her cetological research, leads ultimately to several new experiences and realizations that result in her maturity and enrichment. Seen from this perspective, *The Hungry Tide* appears to embody one of the foremost traits of travel literature[3] as the account of not only the physical travel (mostly by the author) but also an emotional or psychological evolution to be interpreted as a metaphorical journey towards self-discovery. To quote Norman Douglas, a travel narrative entitles the reader "not only to an exterior voyage, to descriptions of scenery and so forth, but [also] to an interior, a sentimental or temperamental voyage, which takes place side by side with the outer one" (quoted in Fussell 203).

Piya's journey, in this sense, can be compared to Graham Greene's experience earned from his journey to Africa as depicted in *Journey without Maps* (1936) wherein the author narrates his experience to be ending in an ordeal exacerbated by fatigue, distress and fever, which finally leads to a moment of epiphanic insight that enables him to sense in himself 'a passionate interest in living', an attainment of self-knowledge akin to 'a conversion' (Greene 201). For Greene, it is a "[S]low foot-sore journey into an interior virtually unknown" (quoted in Fussell 67).

Piya's voyage to the tide country and the experience she gains through her interaction and proximity with Kanai evinces a resemblance to Robyn Davidson's phenomenal travel narrative, *Tracks* (1980). Davidson details her journey across the Australian desert that leads her to the accomplishment of a renegotiation of her Australian identity through the understanding she gains from her encounters with Eddie, an elderly Aborigine man. Similarly, Piya, in the course of her trip through the interiors of the tide country and the interactions with Kanai and Fokir, particularly the latter, re-establishes the link she had lost with her origins. When she returns to Lusibari a fortnight after her departure following the storm, Piya declares that she is going to stay back indefinitely, not as an American but as 'a person of Indian origin' (*Hungry* 425). It is to be noted that Piya instinctively refers to the Lusibari Guest House as 'home' (*Hungry* 427).

Conclusion: Universality Beyond Postcolonial Situation

The Hungry Tide limns the human entity as a tiny and a trifling presence in the massive scheme of things, a member of a 'bewildered' race suffering from its eternal tragedy of rootlessness, of its identity of the 'dispossessed'. *The Hungry Tide* thus draws a sensitive map of the human heart, dotted with crucial events that not only mould the trajectory of the homeward journey but also construct its postcolonial cultural and historical backdrop, thereby scripting a unique discourse of life as an odyssey, the destination of which lies in the confines or the land of one's 'home'.

However, I find the postcolonial tag imposed upon Amitav Ghosh's humane interpretation of the existential crisis of people dislocated from their roots and origins to be one that limits the massive and universal scope of his focus that includes every human individual in every corner of the globe, as articulated in Nirmal's query, "Who are we? Where do we belong?" (*Hungry* 275). An unbiased assessment free from all theorizing makes us realize that Ghose's characters and their complicated existences, their helplessness in respect of the titanic forces of nature, their powerlessness to effect a transformation in their circumstances —all conform to the ultimate existential reality that we humans are nothing more than an insignificant speck in the humongous universe and a mere footnote in the chronicles of existence. It is a truth that will remain unchanged, irrespective of the postmodern or postcolonial or any other theorized identity imposed upon the world, as we remain miserably ignorant, despite the huge mass of knowledge we have acquired, as ever beneath the dark sky and the impenetrable mysteries of existence:

> We've looked and looked, but after all where are we?
> Do we know any better where we are,
> And how it stands between the night tonight
> And a man with a smoky lantern chimney?
> How different from the way it ever stood?
>
> (Frost, "The Star-Splitter" 168)

Notes

1. This rather matter-of-fact interpretation of the concept of home is articulated by Warren, the young husband, to his wife, Mary in Robert Frost's poem, "The Death of the Hired Man" (written in 1905-06, published in 1914 in the volume titled *North of Boston*), where in the course of an evening's conversation they discuss the sudden return of their old farm hand, Silas. Silas, according to Mary, has come back to them because he considers it is his 'home' and 'has come home to die' (Frost 43). It is then that Warren, utters the quoted lines to which Mary gives a more nuanced definition of home:

   > I should have called it
   > Something you somehow haven't to deserve. (Frost 43)

Frost thus underscores what home is supposed to be—something one does not need to deserve, something which naturally belongs to them and vice versa.

2. Almost forty years ago in 1979, one of the murkiest instances of atrocity in Indian history had occurred in the island of Morichjhāpi in the Sundarbans. An enormous community of lower class Hindu citizens of Bangladesh, which had been forced to leave its country, had been settled in Dandakaranya, Madhya Pradesh, but atrocious living conditions as horrific as that of a concentration camp compelled several of them to escape from the camp and to arrive at Morichjhāpi in March 1978 misled by false promises of having a land of their own. The state administration began its desperate attempt to drive away the refugees from January 1979 under the pretext of sustaining the ecological balance and preserving the fauna of the region. In between, the settlers had established almost a country in miniature in the island comprising huts, schools, and even a few innovative means for independent earnings through honest labour. When all measures failed to rupture the resilience of the refugees, the brutal police carnage was unleashed upon the settlers on May 14, 1979 and the entire island was rendered settler-free by May 17, at the cost of thousands of lives and the shattering of countless dreams of a home and a homeland.
3. Travel writing is a flourishing and increasingly popular genre of literary fiction. Initially depreciated as a minor form, travel literature has been growing phenomenally from the latter part of the previous century with the emergence of critically acclaimed travel writers like Paul Theroux, Bruce Chatwin and Robyn Davidson alongside the active patronage of Granta, the prestigious British literary journal. Today, travel literature is regarded as a genre that provides "important insights into the often fraught encounters and exchanges currently taking place between cultures, and into the lies being led, and the subjectivities being formed, in a globalizing world" (Thompson 2). The uniqueness of travel literature, however, consists of the fact that it transcends the conventional confines of the physical journey and maps the emotional and psychological journey that occurs within the author, "an interior, a sentimental or temperamental voyage" (Fussell 203) that leads the author to several significant self-discoveries.

Works Cited

Dattaray, Debashree. "Rethinking Diaspora: A Postcolonial Reading of *The Hungry Tide* and *A Fine Balance*". *Amitav Ghosh: Critical Essays*. Ed. Bibhash Choudhury. 2nd ed. Delhi: PHI Learning, 2016. Print.

Ferdous, Hasan. "The Chronicle Interview: Amitav Ghosh: *The Hungry Tide*". http://www.un.org/pubs/chronicle/2005issue4/0405p48htmlpara2. Web. 15 Sep. 2017.

Frost, Robert. "The Death of the Hired Man". *Collected Poems, Prose, and Plays*. Ed. Richard Poirier and Mark Richardson. 8th ed. USA: The Library of America, 1995. Print.

———. "The Star-Splitter". The Poetry Foundation. https://www.poetryfoundation.org/poems/44273/the-star-splitter. Web.

Fussell, Paul. *Abroad: British Literary Travelling Between the Wars*. Oxford: OUP, 1980. Print.

Ghosh, Amitav. *The Hungry Tide*. Gurgaon: Ravi Dayal and Penguin/Viking, 2008. Print.

———. *The Imam and the Indian*. Gurgaon: Ravi Dayal and Penguin/Viking, 2008. Print.

Greene, Graham. *Journey without Maps*. 1936. London: Vintage Books, 2006. Print.

Mullaney, Julie. *Postcolonial Literatures in Context*. UK: Continuum Books, 2010. Print.

Rushdie, Salman. *Imaginary Homelands: Essays and Criticism: 1981-1991*. London: Granta, 1991. Print.

Thompson, Carl. *Travel Writing*. London: Routledge, 2011. Print.

8

Run Forrest Run: To Home and Away

Susmita Paul

Merriam-Webster Dictionary defines homes as:

> One's place of residence/ the social unit formed by a family living together/ congenial environment/ a place of origin/ an establishment providing residence and care for people with special needs.

In these different interpretations of the same word, two concepts are common. These are—home is a place (it may not be a physical place) with which one is familiar and home as an enclosure for comfortable habitation. Home may be a structure, made of either concrete walls or abstract ideas, but a structure nonetheless. It is something that accommodates one, entertains his/her needs and asks for his/her attachment, empathy and responsibility. Even if the structure is a fluid cultural phenomena, one inhabiting it, must take the responsibility of its outcome. Home has a sense of ownership attached to it too. One must have some kind of ethical or legal rights on the structure called home. It is a socio-spatial system where one's rightful ownership of a certain space matters. But as the case is, without the emotionally pregnant experiences, 'home', as we call it, will be impossible. Therefore, we may say that our 'home' is made up of linguistic representation of the feelings and emotions with respect to a certain time and space. Craig Gurney sees home as an ideological construct created for peoples' "emotionally charged experiences of where they happen to live" (Gurney, 1990: 28). But this argument also has many loopholes. First of all, home as an ideological entity does not always agree with the territorial interpretation of home. On the other hand, if home is merely an abstract concept, then the concept of ownership of home becomes problematized. Again, if home is only an ideological construct, then it becomes useless to ask if anyone does or does not have a physical home. Gurney also opined that those who do not have a fixed home, like the street dwellers, may have a much stronger ideology of 'home' or attachment to where they live. Thus, Gurney believed that:

> ...the cultural milieu of life on the street became a means of redefining home. (Gurney, 1990: 23)

Home is basically an image constructed with language. As we are born into language, all our experiences and feelings are shaped with the clay of language. Derrida says:

> There is no society without writing (without genealogical mark, accounting, archivalization), not even any so-called animal society without territorial mark. ("The Almost Nothing of the Unpresentable", 84)

In "...That Dangerous Supplement..." Derrida made a historical statement "There is nothing outside the text." Here text becomes the universal container, something that we live in. Home is also textually created and possesses structural intricacies as text. Therefore, we may say that, home is an ideological construct, created and relished only through language. And most importantly, our home is somewhere where we don't presently belong. To cherish a dream, we need to detach it from our reality, as reality cannot be fantasized. So, the ideal home should be too idealistic to achieve.

Forrest Gump, the novel by Winston Groom, shows how our concept of home is one big falsehood created by society, politics, economy, culture and other governing institutions. One may dream of belonging to some place, but his dream and actuality have a gap in between that can be crossed only in fantasy. America, at the time of Forrest's childhood saw the emergence of the phenomena called the 'American Dream'. It was a time, when America, in spite of its internal disputes was trying to emerge as an economic giant. It needed to put up an image to the other inferior countries to maintain its tower of capitalism. In order to invite foreign investment and consumerism, America needs to advertise an attractive lifestyle or an ideal home. *Forrest Gump* unveils the internal emptiness of this pretence.

The American Dream—As an Alternative 'Home'

The American hero, if we notice minutely, is often a commoner, someone who is definitely not heroic or blue blooded, but one who raises his/her station in life with efforts and endeavours. If we take *David Copperfield* and *The Great Gatsby* as the epitomes of British and American literature respectively, we may identify the differences more clearly. Unlike David, Gatsby had no family name but became a name himself only to be merged into oblivion. The identity of Gatsby the person was concealed behind the mist of a dream—the dream of a perfect American hero. The American hero does not have a fixed identity (read home). Take Gatsby for example, he has a former life which he deserted for Daisy and he seems to be enacting the role of a millionaire. Throughout his life, he looks for comfort, settlement, and family only to know that he doesn't belong to them. The American hero has to embody the American dream which is no doubt a sham.

The word American Dream was first used by historian James Truslow Adams in his book *Epic of America* who defined it as:

> The American Dream is that dream of a land in which life should be better and richer and fuller for everyone, with opportunity for each according to ability or achievement.

As the name suggests, 'American Dream' is a goal set for a better national life, a target pre-decided to fulfil all the criteria of a bulging nation. French historian Alexis de Tocqueville called it "the charm of anticipated success" (*Democracy in America*). American literature creates heroes who cannot form their home in order to fit in the shoe of that 'American Dream'. They cease to be themselves in order to be what the nation wants them to be. The word 'dream' implies that the concept of American identity is actually a myth; it is yet to come true. The cultural home that America can claim as its pride, is fleeting and yet to settle at a point. The nation itself has formed itself from the debris of a ravished ancient culture and territory only to become the nation of cultural amalgamation. Since then, it had suffered several issues like Civil Rights Movement, Civil War, World War, Cold War, The Great Depression and such others. When *Forrest Gump* was penned, America, while trying to cope up with its difficulties, was adamant to sustain its identity as a global superpower. To do that, it needed stories, legends and myths. The nation was formed by the homeless settlers of Britain who were looking for a home for their sake. In the Newfoundland they created a new home (like New York, New Jersey, etc.) driving out the aboriginals whose homes they destroyed. To be a superpower or to pretend to be one, puts the nation in question under constant pressure which leads to self-denial, myth making and rootlessness. When the nation itself is in such a pathetic state of homelessness, how can a commoner be comfortable in his life? As we have already discussed, most American novels show the journey of the protagonist (not merely physical journey) in search of the unattainable and as destined, the journey leads them to the realization that the goal was just a mirage, what is worthwhile is the journey.

The initial samples of American literature portray the protagonist as under a constant quest. In James Fennimore Cooper's 1826 novel *The Last of the Mohicans*, we may find the journey, the adventure of knowing a newly discovered place and its regions. In Melville's *Moby Dick*, we may find the theme of a quest, a journey seeking the unknown and unexperienced, parallel to that of Columbus. Significantly Captain Ahab has no attachment with his 'home' and family, and the sea appears to be more familiar to him. We may notice a significant change of attitude towards home in American literature if we arrange it chronologically. In the novels of Mark Twain about two young boys we can see through the restlessness of nineteenth century America. The nation has created a 'home' in Newfoundland and was able to gain independence even at that pre-French Revolution era. But the settlement may not be strong enough. The home they have made might not satisfy their dreams and they crave for a new one. So, the quest continues, but in an entirely different manner. At the beginning of the twentieth century, emerges a new concept of home which is celebrated in *The Great Gatsby* by F. Scott Fitzgerald, an ideal product of the Jazz age. The story is set in an imaginary town called the West Egg, thereby emphasizing the impossibility of 'American Dream'. The novel owns a celebrated line:

> So we beat on, boats against the current, borne back ceaselessly into the past. (*The Great Gatsby*)

Written at a time when America has established itself in the global scenario and is looking forward for a better tomorrow, the novel shows that the concept of 'American Dream' is constantly haunted by the past legacy of homelessness. Other American novels that problematizes the concept of home are those of the Beat Generation (like *On the Road, Naked Lunch*, etc.), *The Catcher in the Rye* by Salinger, Ralph Ellison's *The Invisible Man*, John Updike's *Rabbit Run* are worth mentioning.

At a time when the 'American home' should be secure, we may notice an acute insecurity regarding shelter, regarding 'home'. Steinbeck's *The East of Eden* satirizes the Biblical myth of family bonding. The nation has built a home for itself but can't live in it happily. But it is too ashamed to divulge its discomfort to the world and lives a life of pretence which is repeatedly attacked with the weapon of satire. The modern and postmodern American literature bluntly reveals the secrets of American existence and *Forrest Gump* is the general in the army of satirists.

Quest for Home

Forrest was named after a southern Civil War hero Nathan Bedford Forrest, who died like a martyr to secure his home (read homeland). But unlike his namesake Forrest's attachment to his homeland was challenged by various external agencies. His own mental retardation and low IQ damaged his affinity with the surroundings. He can't keep pace with the level of communication of modern society. He seems to be an outcast in the society of smarter folks, therefore, he is denied of one of his potential homes.

> At first, when I's growin up, she'd let me go out an play with everbody, but then she foun out they's teasing me an all, an one day a boy hit me in the back with a stick wile they was chasin me an it raised some fearsome welt. After

> that, she tole me not to play with them boys anymore. I started tryin to play with the girls but that weren't much better, cause they all run away from me. (Groom, *Forrest Gump*, p. 2)

Forrest was named after a person who died for an idea and he himself was completely nulled of any idea whatsoever that could accommodate him. Forrest's thoughts and ideas are principally physical and slightly emotional, thereby ever-changing. He never dwells on a principle for long. He mingled with the Hippie band players, with the soldiers at barracks, with college football buddies, with aboriginals and even with film stars and apes—but none of their ideologies could become his 'home'. Thereby showing that the existence of any ideological 'home' in the then America was illusive.

Forrest's intellectual 'home' was made impossible when he was born with low IQ. In a school for normal kids, he was bracketed as 'Dumbo' and on being sent to an institution for kids like him, he found himself in midst of strange creatures. Being outside the norm, he could have created an alternate identity of 'abnormal' but he seems to be not at ease with the community of "not so normal." He has even created the identity of an 'idiot' for himself, only to break it several times, like getting medal of honour in war, scoring good in Intermediate Light, escaping the aboriginals and evolving as a chess player. Even the identity of an "idiot savant" (that sounds like 'Noble Savage') could not stick to him for long. He even cites a list of idiotic characters found in classics as if creating a league for him:

> Now I know somethin bout idiots. Probly the only thing I do know bout, but I done read up on em—all the way from that Doy-chee-eveskie guy's idiot, to King Lear's fool, and Faulkner's idiot, Benjie, an even ole Boo Radley in To Kill a Mockingbird—now he was a serious idiot. The one I like best tho is ole Lennie in *Of Mice and Men.* (Groom, *Forrest Gump,* 1)

His mother tried hard to spare him the risk of warfare with the help of his idiocy but the state seems not to ponder much on social stratification at the time of political crisis.

Forrest could be at home with his language, but that possibility has also been shattered. There is actually very slight difference between his spoken and written languages. He writes just as he pronounces and seems not to care much about the grammatical rules. Rules, just like the laws, are the social boundaries (if not home) or structures that contain individuals. He notes down the thought in whichever form it comes to him without chaining it in the cell of a certain language. Forrest is not accustomed to the situational use of language. When he is asked to deliver a thank you speech before a congregation, he says "I've got to pee." He is unaware of the fact that language makes meaning only in a certain context. The situational aspect of language ironically benefitted him when during a senatorial campaign Forrest's urge to urinate became an anti-corruption slogan, an epitome of the world's need of purgation. If home could be defined as a context, then Forrest must be lacking one.

The secure domestic life seems not to be Forrest's cup of tea as he takes to roaming almost throughout America. Although he didn't leave Alabama by choice, he could have returned earlier—but he willingly stayed away. In a way, he followed Jenny everywhere, but perhaps Jenny was only a "call of the wild" for him. Her character, her lifestyle was always a foil to Forrest who tried to follow her, imitate her, and accompany her. But when the same Jenny, tired of her rootlessness, wished to settle down, Forrest seemed to have no interest. Dan, similarly, was a homeless fellow and perhaps because of that Forrest was fascinated with him. At the end of the novel, Forrest became a home-giver, as he involved almost everyone he knew since his childhood in the shrimp business and gave all of them not only a secure job, but also a social status, identity and a sense of belongingness. Even Jenny got married and was blessed with motherhood. Jenny's motherhood, again ironically, was caused by Forrest. Forrest is the one who made Jenny abandon her wayward lifestyle, but he himself could never settle down. Like the Orangutan Sue who stayed with him till the last scene, Forrest almost remained rootless.

The nation could never become a 'home' in *Forrest Gump*. While a home is a place of security, shelter, where one is supposed to feel protected and safe, the nation instead pushes the innocent youths like Forrest, Dan or Bubba into the dangerous warfare. Probably the greatest irony is placed on the portion of warfare in the novel. When Bubba died, the last word he murmured was 'home'. May be he wished to go 'home' or he might be actually found his 'home'. As the nation has eventually destroyed the lives of the boys, they discovered their 'home' in death—a place for perpetual solace. The nation valued more the retards like Gump for warfare as the thinkers could be problematic. A statement of Sergeant Kranz is worth mentioning here:

> 'Gump', he says, 'you are not the smartest feller I have ever had, but you is one hell of a soldier. I wish I had a hundrit like you.' (*Forrest Gump,* 28)

Even the dead Bubba was not spared the irony of war, as when Forrest requested Kranz to carry him (his dead body) safely in a helicopter, he replied:

> What the hell—we will even get him accommodations in first class. (*Forrest Gump,* 28)

The state even washed its hands off the responsibilities of the wounded soldiers, as Dan, who was burnt up into a tanker and had deadly injuries, was removed from the hospital before he knew it himself and had no time to bid goodbye to his inmate Forrest. The medal of honour was also satirized as it was later used by Forrest to injure a clerk of the US senate. When the state tried to encash the situation of honouring the soldiers into making more people enlist in the army, Forrest delivered his actual view on war:

> It is a bunch of shit. *(Forrest Gump,* 35)

When Gump was sent to China for a friendly Ping-Pong match, the diplomatic relationship between the countries was laid bare. When Forrest saved Chairman Mao from drowning, Mister Wilkins explained that the state would wish otherwise:

> ...do you not realize that the best thing that could of happened for the United States was to let that sumbitch drown! (*Forrest Gump,* 38)

The state even tried to strangle the protest against the meaningless Vietnam War by hook or crook and whoever challenged it was rendered either criminal or insane. The state treated Forrest as an animal as he was denied all choices and was forced to go to space for an experiment by NASA. On coming back, he received a ritualistic welcome, but the diplomacy underneath was not missed even by Forrest. When the same simpleton Forrest became rich out of his shrimp business, the state began to adore him and even gave him candidature for senatorial election. Thus, the state fails its citizens again and again. The nation is an ideological construct which is governed by the state. To function the state uses social, religious, economic and political propagandas which define the characteristics of a nation. A nation can become an ideal shelter if the policies and interests of the state and its government are designed for the welfare of its people. But in *Forrest Gump,* the case is remarkably otherwise. Here the state manipulates both the concept of the nation and nationalism and the illusion of 'home' is a part of their apparatus.

In the novel, if any character is actually like Forrest, it is the ape Sue. Sue was uplifted from his root by force, had a sad love life and even attempted in vain to go back to his root. Like Forrest, he also had an eventful but unsatisfied life. Sue by choice, went back to the jungle, but could not stay there for long and had to come back to the civilized world once again. Life took unexpected turns for both Sue and Forrest and they ended up being nowhere in each other's company.

Major Fritch was another interesting character in the novel. She was an unmarried, middle aged and astronaut, dissatisfied with her life and complaining about almost everything. The same woman found peace in life among the aboriginals in New Guinea. She even developed an affair with a native Grurck and chose to stay with him instead of returning to what should be her inherited 'home'. She dreamt of having a family life in the wilderness. She found comfort in a place where she must be utmost uncomfortable. The irony is targeted at the grandeur of American identity as a thoroughly American lady prefers the life of a native over the city life. But the case that could have been a perfectly romantic one is problematized with its interpretation given by the state. Besides, the American Government seems to be using this woman, Forrest, and the ape as scapegoats for their experiments. Their lives seem to have no value to their nation as instead of a tamed female ape, they were forced to accept a wild male ape, and the rescue team arrived almost a year late. American dream must be well off, without these problematic folks who always pose a question mark to its relevance.

American diplomacy is again criticized through the character of Sam, an aboriginal living amidst the jungles of New Guinea. Sam can speak English fluently and reveals that he was recruited by the American army against the Japanese. He was trained to speak in English and was also given military training and proper education. After that he was placed into his native people in order to prepare them as guerrilla warriors against Japan. In Big Sam, his American identity and his native identity have a constant clash. Like the civilized countries, he wants his motherland to be blessed with advanced agriculture. To serve his ends, he even employs the diplomacy that he had learnt from the Americans. In spite of being a cannibal, he has not forgotten his civilized etiquettes and tries to stab the group of Americans from behind. It is difficult to denote which actually is the home to him as he exploits both simultaneously. Sam is a person who has eventually lost both his homes and now he knows only one shelter, and that is power. Wherever he is, he wishes to stay powerful as it makes him feel homely.

The question of nation and nationality will be evoked once again on watching the film adaptation of the novel in question, as it has become an inspired work rather than an adaptation. The inherent rootlessness of the novel is remarkably transformed into a sense of belongingness in the film. Thus, the nation shows us what it wants us to see. The definition of home with which we have started our paper, therefore, does not fall in place anywhere in *Forrest Gump*. The home that Forrest was looking for was obviously not a place of living, but a place of being. If home is a social structure, then the person needs to structure himself/herself first as per the demands of the society to be eligible to inhabit the structure. When the structure becomes more important than the people, it is bound to lose its validity. In a way, Forrest Gump is an indicator that the myths behind American dream, American pride and American culture are all fabricated and if Forrest can actually discover an ideal 'home', it will be nowhere but in fantasia.

Works Cited

Adams, James Truslow. *Epic of America*. New Brunswick: Transaction Publishers, 2012. Print.

Cooper, James Fennimore. *The Last of the Mohicans*. London: Penguin Books, 2007. Print.

Derrida, Jacques. *Of Grammatology*. Trans. Gayatri Chakravorty Spivak. Baltimore: John Hopkins University Press, 1976. Print.

Derrida, Jacques. *Points...Interviews, 1974-94*. Trans. Peggy Kamuf, ed. Elisabeth Weber. Stanford: Stanford University Press, 1995. Print.

Dickens, Charles. *David Copperfield*. Birmingham: Konemann UK Ltd., 2000. Print.

Fitzgerald, F. Scott. *The Great Gatsby*. Stuttgart: Klett-Sprachen, 2012. Print.

Groom, Winston. *Forrest Gump*. New York: Washington Square Press, 2002. Print.

Gurney, Craig. "The Meaning of Home in the Decade of Owner-occupation: Towards an Experiential Perspective". Working Paper 88. School of Advanced Urban Studies, University of Bristol, 1990. Print.

Melville, Herman. *Moby Dick*. London: Penguin Books, 2002. Print.

Merriam-Webster, Inc. *The Merriam-Webster Dictionary*. Springfield: Merriam-Webster, 2004. Print.

Tocqueville, Alexis de. *Democracy in America*. Trans. Arthur Goldhammer. Boone: The Library of America, 2004. Print.

Twain, Mark. *The Adventures of Huckleberry Finn*. New Jersey: Penguin Books, 2014. Print.

———. *The Adventures of Tom Sawyer*. New Jersey: Penguin Books, 2002. Print.

9

Life's Tentative Journeys: The Fable-Fact Interface in Paulo Coelho's *The Alchemist*

Rudrashis Datta

Paulo Coelho's novel *The Alchemist* (1988)[1] is, at an immediate level, a novel that presents a fable designed as a search for a 'treasure' through a series of journeys. The plot is straight forward in its movement and there is little in terms of complexities that usually come with an extended work of fiction that weaves layers of signification as incidents or events meander through the agency of characters to some finality. In the course of movement of the plot or plots in a conventionally crafted novel, characters grow, evolve, manifest, or occasionally fade into the periphery. The storyline of *The Alchemist* concerns an Andalusian shepherd boy Santiago's quest for a treasure that is prophesied to be found at the pyramids in Egypt. Most of the novel revolves around his journey for the treasure from his native southern Spanish town to Tangier, his meeting the old 'king of Salem' who presents him with two stones which would aid his decision-making by offering categorical answers in the positive or negative (though we never get to see how), his employment as a help in a crystal shop, his meeting an Englishman who is supposedly a budding alchemist who is to travel through the Saharan desert to meet a famed alchemist, their journey together as a part of a large group crossing the Sahara, their stay at an oasis where Santiago happens to meet Fatima, an Arab girl who is a native in the oasis and for whom Santiago develops feelings of love, his meeting with the black robed Alchemist and their travel together, his epiphany at the pyramids and the final return to his native Spanish town where he actually finds the treasure.

Apparently, there is little in the novel to suggest that Santiago develops or evolves as a character in any comprehensive sense other than the obvious maturity that comes to a well-travelled person who usually learns the importance of following one's dreams while negotiating life's numerous and often unexpected curves. The fact that Coelho often brings in characters to serve specific situations in the plot and pushes them to periphery with little preparation or notice is perhaps the reason why the novel is charged as a 'self-help' text than novel proper.[2] The unconvincing way in which the Englishman and Fatima are pushed outside the scope of the novel serves as an important reminder to the reader that for Coelho, nothing matters more than Santiago's search for the treasure, not even the black-robed Alchemist on whom the work is named. The final meeting of Santiago and his Englishman friend is as unexpected as it is insignificant, plot-wise. Apparently, searching for the Englishman, Santiago finds his tent where the Englishman is shown to be burning out the sulphur in a wood-fuelled furnace. Coelho says,

> He continued to feed the fire, and the boy stayed on until the desert turned pink in the setting sun. He felt the urge to go out into the desert, to see if its silence held the answers to his questions. He wandered for a while, keeping the date palms of the oasis within sight. (94)

These lines are the last to refer to the Englishman friend of Santiago. The neglect of the Englishman is stark, profound and telling and the reader may even be wondering why he was brought into the novel in the first place. In any case, the Englishman, with his books of alchemy does not appear to belong to the same level of depth as alchemy is approached in the novel. He is unfavourably contrasted to Santiago and the Alchemist, with categorical and strategically placed nuances that place his approach to alchemy as distinctly 'physical', being limited to mastery of books and the search for the elixir or stone which would either infuse immortality or turn base metals into gold. It is indeed ironical that long after the Englishman is dismissed from the plot of the novel, the Alchemist turns to the same stone to turn the metal lead into a golden plate, gifting half of it to Santiago partly to make up for the loss he had earlier incurred and partly to compensate him for a robbery he is fated to undergo soon. In fact, the final drift of the novel is characterized by a brand of the use of alchemy that is purposive, physical and mundane. The import of the irony in the calculation of the parting gift of the Alchemist can hardly be missed:

> They returned to the gates of the monastery. There, the alchemist separated the disk into four parts. "This is for you," he said, holding one of the parts out to the monk. "It's for your generosity to the pilgrims." ....The alchemist turned to the boy. This is for you. To make up for what you gave to the general.... "And this is for me," said the alchemist, keeping one of the parts. "Because I have to return to the desert, where there are tribal wars." He took the fourth part and handed it to the monk. "This is for the boy. If he ever needs it." (147-48)

For the man who taught Santiago to hear the 'Soul of the World' and act accordingly, the final gesture in the novel appears to undo the evolution he had supposedly made as an Alchemist through a gradual but definite movement from the physicality of alchemy to its abstraction and spirituality.

Fatima's disappearance in the novel is equally unsettling. Having sustained most of Santiago's attention and emotion during the stay in the Saharan oasis, it is a surprise that Santiago's resolve to return to Fatima in the oasis wavers with the Alchemist advising him to move forward without considering a life with Fatima. The Alchemist says,

> You must understand that love never keeps a man from pursuing his destiny. If he abandons that pursuit, it's because it wasn't true love...the love that speaks the Language of the World. (115)

Santiago's reaction to these words is uncharacteristically passive. The Alchemist goes unchallenged even though his argument illogically pits love against destiny, and Fatima suddenly becomes a character whose presence in the novel would appear to pose an ideological counter-points to the Alchemist's control of Santiago's thought. For nearly a third of the novel thereafter, Fatima is virtually forgotten.

The ideological crisis the novel suffers from is as much sourced in its plot as in its professed philosophy. While Coelho takes recourse to the time tested fable paradigm of a journey or a quest and the inevitable presence of the 'wise old man' motif, Santiago being the classic hero and the Alchemist being the guiding wise man, the manner in which Santiago is shown to blunder and suffer from infirmities while on the quest makes his victory at the end of the novel unconvincing and tentative. The reader cannot miss the coincidences during critical crises in the plot. The chance encounters with tribesmen happen just at the point the plot appears to lose its way. The 'figures' which appeared before Santiago as he was digging the sand near the pyramids had their backs to the moonlight and he could see "neither their eyes nor their faces" (154). They turn out to be refugees from the tribal wars who are in need of money. After Santiago is robbed of whatever he could find with his hard digging, one of them appear to be an alter ego of Santiago who happened to refuse to travel a reverse path to wealth. He tells Santiago,

> You're not going to die. You'll live, and you'll learn that a man shouldn't be so stupid. Two years ago, right here on this spot, I had a recurrent dream, too. I dreamt that I should travel to the fields of Spain and look for a ruined church where shepherds and their sheep slept. In my dream there was a sycamore growing out of the ruins of the sacristy, and I was told that, if I dug at the roots of the sycamore, I would find a hidden treasure. But I'm not so stupid as to cross an entire desert just because of a recurrent dream. (155)

The fact that Santiago is shown to return to his homeland and find the treasure at the exact spot where the refugee dreamt the treasure was, is an illustration of the tentative nature of the 'following the dream' philosophy of Coelho. Clearly, the treasure that is prophesied to Santiago in the Egyptian pyramids is less of a material hoard and more of the knowledge of where the treasure actually is. Essentially, the epilogue of the novel is a homecoming for Santiago. His final complaint on the supposed futility of his travel is essentially the complaint of the typical reader. If Santiago had to find the treasure in his own backyard, why was he made to experience the uncertain and hazardous network of a complex journey to the pyramids and back? The reply of the voice on the wind is apparently that of Coelho—"If I had told you, you wouldn't have seen the Pyramids. They're beautiful, aren't they?" Clearly, therefore, Santiago is positioned as an exact opposite of Veronika in Coelho's *Veronika Decides to Die*. While much of Santiago's journey carries the hazard of an unsure and perplexed traveller who is carried away more through circumstances than free-will, the lack of variety and movement is the very reason Veronika appears to be tired of life to the extent of seeking an escape through death.

At the level of popular philosophy, Coelho negotiates a complex maze of cross connecting paths between belief, credibility and spirituality. While the novel does not offer anything new in the manner in which the fable of self-discovery is handled with the usual motifs of a hero on a journey, the guidance of an old man who is experienced enough to make up for the hero's lack of knowledge and tact, and recurrent appearances of dreams or omens, *The Alchemist* offers a fresh perspective on what constitutes a 'home' in popular literature. At the literal level, a 'home' is more of a culturally conditioned socio-spatial construct which serves both to shelter families and to isolate them. Conveniently, a 'home' is a society at a micro-cosmic level. Increased mobility at both horizontal and vertical levels have since replaced the literal concept of a home with an ideologically conditioned reference point, the crux being that home is both literal and figurative. At the figurative level, a 'home' would ideally carry with it the sub-text of a journey's beginning and its completion, and the journey could be physical or spatial or more often ideological or evolutionary.[3] Judged in this context, Santiago's journey and his apparent lack of a 'home' in its obvious physical sense is made to be compensated through the evolved ideology of the Alchemist who initiates Santiago into believing that so long as he is listening to the 'voice of the world', the world as a whole would be his home. In fact, the only point of ideological difference in what should ideally constitute a 'home' in the novel appear to come when Santiago's journey for the treasure is seriously threatened by his attraction for Fatima in the oasis and his deep-seated urge to settle at the oasis with her. The Alchemist, tactful enough not to put Fatima at the opposite pole of the boy's search for treasure, actually blends the seemingly diametrical ideologies of starting a family and a home, and continuing with the quest, into a single purpose inspiration of existence for Santiago, his argument being that he would get Fatima's love and respect only if he continues in his quest. The novel's final words come through Santiago's triumphant exclamation, "I'm coming, Fatima" (161). Whether Santiago's professed declaration is the beginning of yet another journey on a different plane of living is difficult to tell, but the weakness he has for continuing with varied shades of journeys cannot be missed. Even if he begins another journey to the oasis for Fatima, Coelho makes it apparent that having discovered his powers of reading the voice of the world, Santiago is perhaps prepared to undertake this journey alone, in much the same manner as Gabriel Garcia Marquez's Blacaman the Good attains extraordinary powers through a complex process of initiatory experiences by his mentor. If *The Alchemist* ends with the promise of another journey of the protagonist, we are sure that unlike the previous quest which was a passive boy's negotiation with a string of circumstances inspired through external sources and mechanisms of plot, his second journey would be that of one who is best equipped to move towards a purposive quest for the ideal home in the oasis. Even if he finds one, we are unsure whether Santiago would turn into another Veronika, who has everything going on perfectly for her, and yet she decides to die, overdosing on sleeping pills. At the level of plot, Coelho seems to keep this fable-fact interface tentative in *The Alchemist* by occasionally putting Santiago through emotions of self-pity and distrust of one's surroundings. The realism of Santiago's epiphany after being cheated of all the money that he had can hardly be missed. In a moment of acute depression and helplessness, Santiago sinks into a monologue that pits his misery and loneliness with an unsympathetic and careless world:

> When I had my sheep, I was happy, and I made those around me happy. People saw me coming and welcomed

> me, he thought. But now I'm sad and alone. I'm going to become bitter and distrustful of people because one person betrayed me. I'm going to hate those who have found their treasure because I never found mine. And I'm going to hold on to what little I have, because I'm too insignificant to conquer the world. (37)

In an interview, Coelho spoke of his commitment to a literature that shows 'man in search of his own identity' and his political attitude is antithetical to the prevailing attitude of 'dying alive'. He feels that "people end up dying to the world on the day they renounce their dreams."[4] As a philosophical proposition, his thesis is neither new nor ideal, for the thesis borders on optimism as an ideological construct, and as his novel shows, dreams can be notoriously dangerous to be followed if they begin and end with shallow, selfish considerations of the physicality of human existence. *The Alchemist* shows that all journeys are tentative and the search for the ideal home is an exercise in perpetuity and is therefore essentially incomplete. Coincidences and accidents make up most of the journey Santiago undertakes in the novel, and as human beings are a function of shifting identities and searching such identities would be a compulsory negotiation of conflicting pulls, it is unclear how Santiago can be a role model in our life's journeys or mankind's search for an ideal home. The conflicting inherent in the clinching realization of Santiago that "men dream more about coming home than about leaving" and the finality of the Alchemist's declaration—"You are almost at the end of your journey. I congratulate you for having pursued your destiny" can hardly be missed (118-19). The fact that this conflict is left unresolved is perhaps the reason for the novel's success as popular fiction since it gives readers the privilege of filling the empty dots of unresolved quests and incomplete journeys with a rare sense of freedom of the imagination.

Notes

1. Originally written in Portuguese with the title *O Alquimista* in 1988, the novel was translated into English in 1993.
2. The interpretation of *The Alchemist* as a 'self-help' text gained currency following Gregory Cowles' review of the novel for *The New York Times* on 8 October 2009 and since then the

novel has been categorized more as popular philosophy than mainstream fiction.

3. Martin Heidegger is possibly the first modern philosopher to interrogate the concept of the 'home' in the contemporary context of existentialist philosophy in *Being and Time*.
4. See Glauco Ortolano.

Works Cited

Coelho, Paulo. *The Alchemist: A Fable about following your Dream*. Noida: HarperCollins Publishers, 1993. Print.

———. *Veronica Decides to Die: A Novel of Redemption*. Noida: HarperCollins Publishers, 2006. Print.

Cowles, Gregory. *The New York Times Sunday Book Review*—'Base Metal into Gold', 8 October 2009. http://www.nytimes.com/2009/10/18/books/review/InsideList-t.html?scp=6&sq=the%20alchemist%20paulo%20coelho&st=cse [Accessed 7 July, 2017]. Web.

Heidegger, Martin. *Being and Time*. (Trans. Stambaugh, Joan), New York: State University Press, 1996. Print.

Marquez, Gabriel Garcia. *Leaf Storm and Other Stories*. "Blacaman the Good, Vendor of Miracles" (113-22) (Trans. Gregory Rabassa). New York: Harper and Row Publishers, 1972. Print.

Ortolano, Glauco. "An Interview with Paulo Coelho—The Coming of Age of a Brazilian Phenomenon". *World Literature Today*, pp. 57-59, April-June 2003. Print.

10

The Ones Who Fell Through: Home of the Dispossessed in Arundhati Roy's *The Ministry of Utmost Happiness*

Arpa Ghosh

In the Dantesque version, the Achean hero Ulysses urges his faithful mariners to set out from home in search of new life-enhancing, adventures. Home, with its small, sequestered, routine-bound existence, is anathema for the hero of *Odyssey* who feels stifled in its confines. The subtext is that the alpha-male Ulysses feels unwanted and superfluous in the Ithacan set-up that is chiefly dominated by his unadventurous administrator-son. Rules and regulations rather than unbridled passion form the staple of Ithaca. Travel is therefore regarded by Ulysses as the obverse of the limited, sheltered and tedious home. Travel is exciting, uplifting and endless. Home is where you dig in roots and live the life of a tree. Travel leads you to spread your wings, experience weightlessness and fly like a bird.

Ulysses's vision of home and travel is undoubtedly patriarchal. Home is tedious because it is a given. Like his family, a hero cannot choose his home. He can only choose to escape from it. Whether he goes or stays, home remains an unvarying constant peopled by loyal women and mediocre progeny.

A novel that problematizes home in the context of travel is Arundhati Roy's *The Ministry of Utmost Happiness*, a novel with a deeply ironical title in which happiness is shown to ultimately reside in a smelly graveyard full of injured animals and denizens who have fallen through—eunuchs, transvestites, petty businessmen, untouchables, criminals, and drug addicts. In the graveyard, the final equalizer and the home of the dead, existence is expanded and deepened spatially,—the graveyard is expansive enough to accommodate human and animal pariahs and recluses,—and temporally,—the past and the present, the living and the dead cohabit peacefully. The graveyard teems with life and history. Personal narratives are embalmed and made part of a special community history. In this unusually packed novel, the reader rather than the characters is taken on a journey that begins in Delhi and fans out to the length and breadth of India: Kashmir in the north, Gujarat in the west and Bastar in the south, to finally return to the graveyard in Purana Delhi.

The narrative is governed by Anjum, a transwoman who has left her father's home voluntarily, and Tilo, an English-speaking architect (a fictional prototype of the author) who has had a traumatic childhood history that leads her away from her foster-mother's home. Both are exiles; Anjum, since she is a hermaphrodite and Tilo because of her disturbed personal history. The limited consciousness third person narration of the novel centers chiefly on these two characters. By choosing them, the author confounds the accepted bourgeois idea of the home as familial hub and refuge from the outset.

For Anjum, the journey from her parental home to Khwabgah (a Hijra quarter in Purana Delhi) and many years later to the graveyard adjoining the hospital in the walled city (which she gradually turns into her new home, Jannat Guest House and Funeral Services) may be territorially short, but it marks a long psychological trajectory. From misfit and a 'son' of whom 'his' parents are ashamed and guilt-ridden, Anjum matures into a care-giver, provider of shelter and hostess of a graveyard-guesthouse. Remarkably, there is no attempt to sensationalize or render exotic Anjum's role. Her sexual life is absent from the narrative, whereas in Jeet Thayil's *Narcopolis* and Khushwant Singh's *Delhi* the cruelty and abuse associated with a eunuch's sexual life are strongly focused upon. Since Arundhati's agenda is political rather than personal, *The Ministry of Utmost Happiness* showcasing almost all the major political upheavals beginning with Godhra and ending with the rapes of *adivasi* women in Bastar, Anjum is awarded the status of a witness rather than victim. Also in Anjum's case, there are reversals of roles. Saddam Hussain, an untouchable disguised as Muslim, an unusually resourceful man who has the solution to all problems troubling the dispossessed, is Puck to Anjum's Oberon. The empowerment of the hermaphrodite in a mixed community, albeit a community of the dispossessed and proletariat, is indeed a novelty as in previous novels such as Khushwant Singh's *Delhi* and Jeet Thayil's *Narcopolis* the eunuch has been represented as a victim-figure of an essentially patriarchal set-up.

Roy's vision is as empowering as it is exhilarating. Cooperation rather than competition characterize the social behavior of the poor and the dispossessed as is evinced in every page of the novel.

> Working-class culture, by contrast, was governed by values quite different to those holding sway in capitalism; for example, cooperation rather than competition. (Day, 2001, 192)

The novel illustrates how the underclass, of its own initiative, without minimal help from the state, succeeds in eking out a space and community of its own. The inventiveness, industry and enterprise of Anjum, Saddam and their friends is acknowledged and celebrated by the novel. The authorial disillusion, irony and deep anger are directed against the state that is uniformly indifferent to the plight of its poor, or vicious in its attack of its critics and malcontents, or simply greedy to extract its cuts from the meager of portions of the dispossessed. The anger is expressed in such ironic statements as: "Except in Delhi there was no war other than the usual one—the war of the rich against the poor" (*MUH*, 392); and "So all in all, with a People's Pool (that has no water), a People's Zoo (full of damaged, decrepit animals and birds) and a People's School (with only one teacher), things were going well in the old graveyard. The same however could not be said of the Duniya (the larger world ruled by the State)" (*MUH*, 400).

The State's negative role is highlighted in the callous way in which Musa's baby-daughter, Miss Jebeen, is mowed down by a stray bullet to disperse a death-rally in Kashmir. The Kashmiri

Miss Jebeen's death is counterbalanced by the adoption of an abandoned, black baby by Tilo and Anjum. This baby, off-spring of police gang-rape of a communist *adivasi* worker is named Miss Jebeen by Tilo to commemorate the death of the first child. The role of the State as the slayer of future possibilities, and that of the eunuch community as cherisher of the same is thus driven home.

The burning question under such circumstances is when the national home turns toxic and inimical to the welfare of its unprivileged denizens, what should be the new definition of home or refuge? There are three reigning consciousnesses in the novel: Anjum, Tilo and Biplab. While the bureaucrat Biplab Dasgupta gets stuck in an empty flat unable to identify with the national policies of which he is a part, yet unable to cast his die with the victims of the state, and slowly drinks himself to death, Anjum creates a community home for herself, a Noah's Ark, housing not only her human friends but also an increasing herd of injured and aged animals. Tilo, an educated woman who has friends in influential quarters who rescue her from calamitous situations and welcome her into their fold, is never able to identify with them. Her informed shift to the ranks of the proletariat is a major narrative movement. When she moves into Jannat Guest House permanently: "For the first time in her life, Tilo felt her body had enough room to accommodate all its organs" (*MUH*, 305).

Magic realism adds that extra element of toy-land fantasy and the presentation of the eunuch community as ghostly. Says Anjum at one point: "*Arre*, even we aren't real. We don't really exist" (*MUH*, 84). Towards the end of the novel, referring to Tilo's calm acceptance of Musa's death the author says:

> ...the burden of perpetual apprehension that she had carried around for years—of suddenly receiving news of Musa's death—had lightened somewhat. Not because she loved him any less, but because the battered angels in the graveyard that kept watch over their battered charges held open the doors between worlds (illegally, just a crack), so that the souls of the present and the departed could mingle, like guests in the same party. It made life

> less determinate and death less conclusive. Somehow everything became a little easier to bear. (*MUH*, 398)

Such presentations give the residents an exotic status. This is further enhanced by the author's emphasis that Anjum and her people belong to the Walled City outside Duniya which is puzzling and fearsome in its tendency to exploit, divide and complicate. Occasionally (as in the above passages), the reader could feel that Jannat House is permeated with a different reality, a separate set of laws.

> Magic realists are postcolonials who avail themselves most forcefully of the deices of postmodernism, of pastiche, irony, parody and intertextuality; they are alternatively recognized as oppositional to cultural imperialism, but also as reactionaries, who perpetuate the retention of the Western stereotype of the exotic Other. In other words, magic realism and its associated styles and devices is alternatively characterized as a transgressive mechanism that parodies Authority, the Establishment and the Law, and also as the opposite of these, as a domain of play, desire and fantasy for the Rich and Powerful. (Cooper, 29)

However, in favour of Arundhati it should be mentioned that the writer-activist has a long history of being intimately associated with driven out peoples. She has fought their battles and acted as their spokesperson much to the chagrin and ire of ruling parties who have sought to strengthen the hands of the rich and the powerful at the cost of the poor. Therefore, Ahmed's allegation of what is missing in Salman Rushdie's work cannot really be leveled against Arundhati in quite the same manner:

> ...the dailiness of lives lived under oppression, and the human bonding—of resistance, of decency, of innumerable heroisms of both ordinary and extraordinary kinds—which make it possible for large numbers of people to look each other in the eye, without guilt, with affection and solidarity and humour, and makes life, even under oppression, endurable and frequently joyous. Of that other kind of life his fictions, right up to *The Satanic Verses,* seem to be largely ignorant. (Cooper, 30)

In fact, though, by situating much of the drama in and around a graveyard, the author distances her characters from the educated, upwardly mobile, middle-class reader, her stress is on the 'ordinariness' of Anjum's life: her fears, anxieties, traumas, celebrations and jubilations that are not much different from our lives, does help take away much of Anjum's 'strangeness'. Remarkably, the Marxist touch of Anjum breaking away first from her parental home, and then from the walled eunuch-house of Khwabgah to set up residence in a graveyard and gradually collect a motley gathering of colourful humans and animals questions the hierarchies and exclusionary practices associated with the traditional home and family, undercuts the exoticism of magic realist strategies deployed in the novel.

The carnival has been used as a strong unbroken motif. The locale that reinforces the transgressive, chaotic power of the carnival is Jantar Mantar, a congregation of weird, persistent protestors who mill around wearing their placards and holding up their protest documents. Jantar Mantar with its milling demonstrating crowd, each with a separate issue, is a microcosm of disaffected India. From the Kashmiri Mothers of the Departed to the communist *adivasi* protestors of Bastar: all groups assemble to demonstrate against an increasingly intolerant state. A major figure here is the self-named Dr. Azad Bharatiya (whose PhD is pending), an educated protestor who has been fasting on and off for the last eighteen years and painstakingly preparing his hand-written documents on some issue or the other. At a time when "the food shops are bursting with food" (*MUH*, 99). Azad Bharatiya, by opting to fast and not feast, is projected as the non-conformist resistor.

> Bakhtin describes carnival in all its forms as 'sharply distinct from the serious official, ecclesiastical, feudal and political cult form and ceremonials,' in that 'offerred a completely different, nonofficial, extraeccleiastical and extrapolitical aspect of the world;' it was a second life outside officialdom'. It is laughter that 'gives form to carnival rituals' and which 'frees them completely from all religious and ecclesiastic dogmatism, from all mysticism and piety.' Carnival is sensuous and has a 'strong element of play'.... Bakhtin's carnival is 'a world of topsy-turvy, of heteroglot exuberance, of ceaseless overrunning and

> excess, where all is mixed, hybrid, ritually degraded and defiled.' (Cooper, 1998, 24)

The world of the topsy-turvy, of heteroglot exuberance, of ceaseless overrunning and excess—whether it be in the flowing of *Bakhr Id* sacrificial blood or the gargantuan, gourmet feasts prepared by the eunuchs on religious occasions—is what we get in large portions of the novel.

The comic replaces the age-old horror associated with the life of a hermaphrodite. Chaucerian laughter, gentle and admiring in its keen observation of unusual types, is found in abundance in the portmanteau novel. When to her trusted Man Friday, Anjum muses:

> Once you have fallen off the edge like all of us have, including our Biroo (a badly abused stray dog that Anjum adopts), you will never stop falling. And as you fall you will hold on to other falling people. The sooner you understand that the better. The place where we live, where we have made our home, is the place of falling people. Here there is no *haqeeqat*. *Arre*, even *we* aren't real. We don't really exist. (*MUH*, 84)

Walled within Purana Delhi or housed in the graveyard, the eunuchs are warm, caring folks. Love-affairs are referred to in passing. The lacerating physical exploitation associated with eunuch-existence is omitted from the narrative. Rather, their love for colour, music, festivities, community fellow-feeling and motherly attitude towards children (indicating their deep and burning desire for motherhood) is highlighted. What comes across is the ceaseless joyous energy of people who are largely excluded from mainstream existence. The selective presentation of eunuch-existence provides insight into an alternative *haqeeqat* or reality; one that is studiously glossed over by mainstream society.

If Anjum the eunuch is filled with a burning desire to be a mother, Tilo, the young architect, has essentially given up on desire. It is indicated rather than stated outright that the childhood trauma of being socially rejected by her mother has killed all desire in her of rising in life. Whereas her Bengali bureaucrat friend Biplab Dasgupta, driven by career finally finds himself isolated from friends and family, cooped up in his lonely apartment in a post area in Delhi, Tilo finds meaning and fulfillment in her graveyard life in the Jannat Guest House, acting as the teacher of the children housed there. The trajectory of Tilo, from a rented apartment in post New Delhi to Anjum's graveyard guesthouse, is a reverse arc (the route from failure to success usually portrayed in traditional novels). Tilo's deindividuation actually enhances and deepens the concept of home, giving it a radical Marxist connotation altogether. In the flat below lives a snobbish middle-class woman who treats her underage *adivasi* servant as a slave. On the floor above waits Tilo for a life that will eventually erase all hierarchical differences; a life that will spill over borders and boundaries and construct a home that is collective and cooperative.

The graveyard communal home with its perpetually open doors, its friends and visitors constantly trickling in and out is a wish fulfillment.

> Between Zainab and Saddam, they had turned the graveyard into a zoo—a Noah's Ark of injured animals. There was a young peacock that could not fly, and a peahen, perhaps his mother, who would not leave him. Zainab arrived one day in an autorickshaw with several cages stuffed with three dozen budgerigars that had been absurdly coloured in luminous dyes.... A small tortoise —an abandoned pet—that Saddam had found in a park, with a sprig of clover in one nostril, now wallowed on the terrace in a mud-pit of his own. Payal-the-mare had a lame donkey for a companion. He was called Mahesh.... Biroo (the dog) was getting old, but his and Comrade Laali's progeny had multiplied and they tumbled around the place. Several cats came and went. As did the human guests in Jannat Guest House. (*MUH*, 399)

Home is depicted as being replete with a sense of history; the living sharing their quarters with the dead.

> Over time Anjum began to enclose the graves of her relatives and build rooms around them. Each room had a grave (or two) and a bed....

> Gradually Jannat House became a hub for Hijras who, for one reason or another, had fallen out of, or been expelled from, the tightly administered grid of Khwabgah. (*MUH*, 67-68)

Instead to being upwardly mobile the denizens of Jannat keep extending their varied and heterogenous home by including the lowest of the low.

Travel in this novel is marked by trauma. Associated as it is with the Duniya or the big, bad world, travel experience silences a person. Anjum's return from Gujarat, post riots in which her companion, an aged Muslim gentleman, is hacked to death by Hindus *karsevaks* and she herself is spared only because it is considered bad omen to kill hermaphrodites, leaves her emotionally scarred. She refuses to talk about it and leaves Khwabgah shortly afterwards. We are not told what Anjum thinks about her near-death experience. In fact, the novel opens on an ominous note:

> She lived in the graveyard like a tree....
>
> When she first moved in, she endured months of casual cruelty like a tree would—without flinching.... When people called her names—clown without a circus, queen without a palace—she let the hurt blow through her branches like a breeze and used the music of her rustling leaves as balm to ease the pain. (*MUH*, 3)

It is interesting that branches rather than roots are mentioned. Roots designate stasis, a refusal to cross frontiers and challenge the old order. But branches stand for growth, renewal, shelter and breezinees that can be translated as the sheer joy of life. Says Salman Rushdie:

> In all quests the voyager is confronted by terrifying guardians of territory, an ogre here, a dragon there. So far and no further, the guardian commands. But the voyager must refuse the other's definition of the boundary, must transgress against the limits of what fear prescribes. He steps across the line. The defeat of the ogre is an opening of the self, an increase in what is possible for the voyager to be. (Rushdie, 2003, 409)

Anjum refuses to live as Aftab, the boy her parents crave for and voluntarily crosses over to Khwabgah, the eunuch-quarters. After the Gujarat riots, her first-hand experience of racial hatred leads her to move away from Khwabgah as well. The graveyard with its open space and buried dead finally becomes her home.

Tilo's visit to Kashmir,—the land fighting for its freedom from an intolerant torturer-state,—to meet the love of her life, Musa, the architect turned militant, is fraught with nightmarish experience of the Indian Army's atrocities against Kashmiri civilians. She too returns vibrating with shock and outrage, unable to articulate her experiences. Her other journey to Cochin to care for her dying mother also ends in disaster since her mother's mad, death-bed exclamations bring home to her the old woman's inbuilt aversion for the untouchable and her guilt at having had a child with an untouchable.

Instead of homes, we have two carnivalesque human conglomerates. One is Jannat Guest House, an asylum for tormented, transgenders and rejects from all over the city, an undefined space nurturing motherhood, resistance, protest and community feelings and the other is Jantar Mantar, a never-ending fair of protest inhabited by anti-establishment individuals and groups. The presiding spirit of this medley is Azad Bharatiya, a lovable protestor who has been fasting for over eighteen years over some issue of the other. These spaces have individuals milling around freely. At the same time we get the feeling that these are contained spaces within walled cities tolerated and observed by the establishment.

The Jannat Guest House gradually becomes a shelter for human and animal discards. Failures and misfits literally come here to roost. However, this containment is what is disturbing about the novel. Though it makes for a wonderful read about how Anjum, Tilo and their human and animal friends, dead and alive, live happily ever after, the Jannat Guest House actually performs the function of a comfortable closure to a text with strong anti-establishment and subversive tendencies.

Previous fictional portrayals of eunuchs or transwomen—Bhagmati in Khushwant Singh's novel *Delhi* and Dimple in Jeet Thayil's *Narcopolis*—have dealt largely in voyeuristic portrayals of sexual masochism, torture, victimhood and the like. The eunuchs in such novels are the lowest of the low used and abused across class and status barriers.

In Arundhati's narrative, the eunuch is depicted as the practitioner and inheritor of a clan culture that holds the motley-narrative together. In a world of crumbling certainties, the eunuch-community is the last bastion of harmony and social adjustment. At one level, this is a celebration of wholeness, the hermaphrodite being the possessor male and female genitalia and therefore representing entirety. At another, it is deeply ironic comment on a State that has relinquished all responsibility of its poor, and the poor, deviant and dispossessed are seeking refuge with a past-her-prime penurious hermaphrodite and in fact the hermaphrodite is providing care and refuge to them (roles that an ideal State should perform).

An answer may be runed in the ambiguous identity of the chosen prophet or muse, Hazrat Sarmad Shaheed, of firstly Jahanara Begum, mother of Aftab/Anjum, and later, under Anjum's guidance, the object of worship of the eunuchs.

Sarmad was a Jewish Armenian merchant who travelled from Persia to Delhi in pursuit of Abhay Chand, a young Hindu boy with whom he loved. At first he embraced Islam. But soon his spiritual search compelled him to abandon orthodox Islam. Before an irate orthodox Aurangzeb, when asked to recite the Kalima: *la ilaha illallah, Mohammad-ur rasul Allah*—(There is no God but Allah and Mohammad is his Messenger), Sarmad stopped short after: *la illaha* (there is no God), pleading that until his spiritual quest was complete he was unable to recite the rest of the Kalima and endorse Allah's supremacy. For this he was beheaded by the emperor.

Sarmad's inductive, empirical approach to life sets him apart from the majority of *Pirs* and prophets. The wheel comes full circle with a comfortable, feel-good closure when Anjum takes Saddam and her foster-daughter Zainab to the Hazrat's dargah.

> Sixty years had gone by since Jahanara Begum had taken her son Aftab to Hazrat Sarmad and asked him to teach her how to love him....

> Jahanara Begum's son had become her daughter and [Zainab] was now a bride. But other than that, nothing much had changed....
>
> Anjum said a prayer and asked him to bless the young couple.
>
> And Sarmad—Hazrat of Utmost Happiness, Saint of the Unconsoled and Solace of the Indeterminate, Blasphemer among Believers and Believer among Blasphemers—did. (*MUH*, 416)

Like Theseus, the overbearing Athenian monarch in William Shakespeare's *A Midsummer Night's Dream*, Hazrat Sarmad frames Arundhati Roy's narrative. But there the resemblance ends, for Theseus is a believer of definitive logic and male hierarchy, whereas with Sarmad the only permanence in life is change and flux.

The beauty of the novel perhaps lies in its careful balancing of the definite and the indefinite, closure and open-endedness, carnival and cruelty, magic and heinousness. Sarmad, blasphemer among believers and believer among blasphemers is the chosen muse of the narrative and Anjum, the hermaphrodite, housing in a single body maleness and femaleness, is its apt presiding consciousness.

Works Cited

Bakhtin, M.M. *The Dialogic Imagination: Four Essays*. Ed. Michael Holquist. Trans. Caryl Emerson and Michael Holquist. Austin: The University of Texas Press, 1981. Print.

Cooper, Brenda. *Magic Realism in West African Fiction: Seeing with a Third Eye*. New York: Routledge, 1998. Print.

Day, Gary. *Class: The New Critical Idiom*. London: Routledge, 2001. Print.

Ray, Arundhati. *The Ministry of Utmost Happiness*. Gurugram: Penguin Random House India, 2017. Print.

Rushdie, Salman. *Step Across this Line: Collected Non-Fiction 1992-2002*. London: Vintage, 2003. Print.

Singh, Khushwant. *Delhi*. New Delhi: Penguin Books India Pvt. Ltd., 1990. Print.

Thayil, Jeet. *Narcopolis*. London: Faber & Faber, 2012. Print.

11

Home and Identity in Ritwik Ghatak's Films

Pritha Kundu

In Ritwik Ghatak's *Komal Gandhar*, Bhrigu and Anasuya look over the river Padma, mourning their lost 'home', that is, 'East Bengal', which lies on the other side of the river. That 'home' has now turned into *bidesh*, a foreign country. The trauma of the partition of Bengal which thus affected the Bengali peoples' sense of existence, home and identity, comes recurring in Ritwik Ghatak's films. For his characters, the Radcliffe line is a fatal border that has victimized their lives and living, made them realize how the loss of home and identity could turn down all their hopes and desires.

Ghatak belonged to the generation which had a nostalgic idea of the greater Bengal's cultural identity, and allegiance to undivided Bengal as their 'home'. Even after the partition, people loved to harp on the hope that nothing, however, could belie their homeland's grand narrative of 'imagined togetherness'. There was also a hope among the Bengali refugees that amidst all trials and hardships they would have some kind of peace and shelter in West Bengal, since on both sides of the river exists the 'Bengali' identity. This illusion changed with the passage of time and they began to feel differently, as expressed by the character of Haraprasad in Ghatak's *Subarnarekha*: "We're totally defeated. We can't even commit suicide." Among the pioneering figures of the new wave Bengali cinema, Ghatak, being most deliberately conscious of this polemical geopolitics, could never remain oblivious of this 'betrayal' which made so many people homeless, with their identity at stake. *Meghe Dhaka Tara* has of course received greater attention than his other films concerning such issues. In this paper, the focus will rather be on *Bari Theke Paliye, Subarnarekha,* and *Titas Ekti Nodir Naam*—three films different in approach but all so poignant in depicting the thematic oeuvre of 'home' and 'identity'.

Throughout his film career Ghatak has repeatedly tried to demystify the Partition and its aftermath—communal riots, famine, displacement, rootlessness. The division of the state resulted in the formation of an amorphous, peripheral identity called 'refugee'. In *Bari Theke Paliye*, he makes one of the characters explicitly quote from a poem by Annadashankar Roy, stating that we get annoyed with an innocent child when he/she breaks up a small thing, but we can do nothing when a nation, a state is divided in two, which, in turn, creates a political demarcation between the 'citizen' and the 'homeless', who are in a perpetual exile. In his debut film, *Nagarik*, the discourse of 'homelessness' and 'rootlessness' gets reflected through the problems of accommodation and employment, and the notion of 'home' ultimately gets reduced to a slum. This is further developed in *Bari Theke Paliye*, where the pavement-dwellers ultimately realize that they must accept the footpath as their 'home' in a new state which is not willing to grant them any other right of living and habitation.

Bari Theke Paliye is an adaptation of Shibram Chakrabarty's novella set in pre-Independence Kolkata. The boy-hero, Kanchan, finds his village home claustrophobic and his father's rule oppressive, and runs away to Kolkata. His dream is to grow up, earn money and free his loving yet submissive mother from the patriarchal rule of his father. Ritwik Ghatak in his film version places the story in post-Partition Kolkata. The runaway boy's encounters with a panoramic view of the city—with its streets populated with beggars, thieves, refugees, hawkers, nomadic performers, and his occasional entry into some family spaces within the city, gradually makes him see his own village-home and the position of his parents in a new light. In other words, his experiences in 'exile' gives him new insights into the identity of himself, his father and mother, and prompts his homecoming, at the end. What was originally a child's adventure story, becomes a part of Ghatak's cinematic discourse of identity, both at 'home' and in 'exile'.

Ghatak represents the reality of Partition and unemployment, at best, through the character of Haridas in *Bari Theke Paliye*. Haridas, a former teacher from East Bengal, is now a street vendor in Kolkata. After ten years of futile struggle to get a job, he has now accepted the dual identity of one who is both a seeker and an abandoned. He is constantly in search of her mother who, he believes, like Kanchan, has 'run away' from him. Kanchan, on the other hand, is in search of a mother-figure even in his exile, and this search keeps him bound to the idea of 'home'. The old woman who searches for her own child in every boy of the same age, seems to offer a surrogate home-space to Kanchan—an experience which reinforces the purpose of his journey. Paradoxically, by running away from home, he seeks to reformulate his own identity and idea of 'home' against a backdrop of social unrest, displacement and homelessness posed by the 1943 famine and afterwards, the Partition.

One important way of universalizing the problem of homeless identity, for Ghatak, is to place his characters in the context of modern mythopia. Ghatak's way of storytelling in cinema is often compared to the epic mode, and *Subarnarekha* is one great example of this. In his own words:

> the refugees pose the basic problem in Subarnarekha but the problem of homelessness or rootlessness no more remains confined to the refugee from the partition. I extended it further as an important concept, very apt for the modern man uprooted from his traditional moorings. The geographical sphere is thus merged into a wider generality. (Bannerjee, 68)

In doing so, Ghatak often brings to forefront his female protagonists—to bear much of the pain of homelessness, to take the sufferings of the entire community chiefly on herself, as a 'Mother'-archetype. The juxtaposition 'woman' and 'home' is a common cultural practice in several communities. Thus, the figure of a woman in exile—Ruth amidst the alien corns or Sita in Vanabaas—separated from her familiar surroundings at home, becomes a significant image in literary, mythical and other kinds of narratives that inspires sympathetic responses from the audience. In his book *An Accented Cinema: Exilic and Diasporic Filmmaking*, Hamid Naficy makes an apt observation:

> For the exiles, the house is a site of both deep harmony and hatred.... Significantly, the discourse of memory feminized the house as an enclosure of femininity and domesticity, associated with motherhood and reproduction. This is how many exiles feminize the homeland.... In the accented cinema, the house is an intensely charged place and a signifying trope. (42)

In *Subarnarekha*, the trope of exiled identity is at work from the very beginning. Names are part of identity, and without a name one's claim to identity gets destabilized. As we see in *Bari Theke Paliye*, Kanchan asks a street-boy his name, but he replies, "No, I don't know. Nor do I remember." In *Subarnarekha* (1962), too, names do carry significance, but on an ironic level. The opening scene of the film shows a flag hoisting programme in a school set up in a refugee colony called 'Nabajiban' (new life), at the outskirts of Kolkata. The refugee children from East Bengal have to accept India as their 'new nation' and chant the praise of Bharat Mata under the Indian national flag. Haraprasad tells the assembled party that he will be teaching Bengali and Sanskrit in the school, while Ishwar will take up English and History. The name 'Haraprasad' suggests 'Gift of God', and the man bearing such a name seeks refuge in the idyllic past, in a vain attempt to keep the traditional learning alive. Ishwar, whose name suggests 'God' succumbs to the demand of postcolonial modernity, teaching English and History. In this temporary settlement, which the refugees try to consider as their 'new home', tradition and modernity are thus at play, both threatening and reshaping their identity.

Subarnarekha, being the last film of Ghatak's Partition trilogy, manifests the failure of postcolonial identity-making, with a problematization of the 'home'-idea. It brings into question the elusive concept of finding a "home in exile". Ishwar's sister Sita (bearing the name of the tragic icon of suffering womanhood in the epic *Ramayana*) is doubtful about their "new home", as she asks Haraprasad, "Brother, did you say that we were going to our new home?" Soon we see a low-caste woman called Kausalya along with her son Abhiram (both names are suggestive, again alluded to the *Ramayana*) in search of a shelter. Most ironically, another refugee man turns them away, saying that they are from Pabna, and cannot give shelter to anybody from Dhaka. This discrimination among districts of a nation they have already lost, seems both ridiculous and pathetic. All the more ironical is the implied notion that even in their miserable situation, the Bengali refugees try to maintain their upper-caste bias of sanctity. The entry of a low-born woman will 'pollute' their temporary 'home', which they themselves do not have any right to hold. In a continuation of the scene, both Kausalya and the man refusing her get arrested by the landowner's guard in charge of illegal possession of the land. Without going into theorization, Ghatak clearly depicts through his powerful visual medium how difficult it is to think of the subaltern identity in terms of homogeneity. Poverty, dispossession, homelessness and caste—so many markers there are to destabilize any kind of monolithic identity even for the suffering humanity in general.

Ghatak shows different kinds of de-identification at work. In a colony or slum-like settlement, problems of caste create divisions among the refugees. Abhiram comes under the guardianship of Ishwar. In order to raise her sister along with Abhiram, he leaves the colony and gets a job in Chatimpur, along the river Subarnarekha, which literally means 'the golden line'—carrying a suggestion of hope. With the job comes living quarters, which means a 'home', where Sita and Abhiram grow up together and fall in love. Ishwar is otherwise fond of Abhiram, but when his low-caste identity gets revealed, is unwilling to get his sister married to him. The chief reason behind his opposition to this marriage is something more than his personal caste prejudice: he fears that if his caste-conscious employer comes to know about his connections with Abhiram, he will lose the job; and losing the job means the loss of home.

Unlike Haraprasad, Ishwar is less hopeful about starting a 'new life' by getting stuck in the 'Nabajiban' colony. He instead manages to find a 'home' in Chatimpur, his place of work which eventually gets empty: Sita and Abhiram elope and marry against his will, leaving Ishwar deserted and alone. When Ishwar left the colony, Haraprasad accused him of desertion; but his family, staying on in the settlement, gets nothing better in reward. His wife, unable to bear the semi-starved condition, commits suicide, and Haraprasad comes to haunt Ishwar, with a defeated man's painful 'realization' that self-indulgence, not abstinence, is the way to liberation. As a *doppelganger*, the ghost-like Haraprasad persuades him to undertake a journey to Kolkata, projected as a city of chaos, illicit pleasures and dissolution.

Through the eyes of Ishwar and Haraprasad, we get to see two different sides of Kolkata: on the one hand, there are race-horses and gamblers, a shady nocturnal life populated with people glued to pubs and brothels and on the other, the dehumanized condition of the inhabitants in slums and refugee colonies. In both cases, the formation of a stable human identity is extremely difficult. Earlier in the movie, when in Kolkata, Ishwar tries to get information about Abhiram's lost mother a man in the newspaper office retorts, "A refugee? Who isn't?" Sita's journey from the banks of Subarnarekha to the urban slums of Kolkata, with her husband Abhiram, also reflects a reverse pattern of exilic movements. Unlike her epic/mythical counterpart who chose a life of exile with her husband from the rigid structures of the royal court to the wild, troublesome yet open space of hills and forests, Ghatak's modern Sita spent her childhood first in the refugee colony, then in "the idyllic open structures of home (that) emphasize continuity," and her adulthood suffers in the claustrophobic spaces of a metropolitan slum in Calcutta—"those paranoid structures of exile (that) underscore rupture" (Naficy, 188). At that time, metropolitan cities like Kolkata was swayed by such a tremendous influx of emigrants, and in consequence, a massive want of accommodation and employment, that it was hardly possible for any individual to claim any other identity than that of a refugee.

The bitter cultural truth of loss, waste and dissolution attains to a symbolic and poetic status through Ghatak's thoughtful use of jump-cut shots and montage. Race-horses come out,

Ishwar and Haraprasad drink at a bar, Haraprasad gets drunk and bumps on Ishwar's spectacles and the glasses break, which suggests the complete collapse of sense, rationality and identity of these two men, who began their journey as idealistic teachers. The waiter requests Ishwar to take his companion back to home, and Ishwar retorts, "Home?" Quotes from the *Katha Upanishad* get mixed up with the soft track of Fellini's *La Dolce Vita,* which ends up in Ishwar's meeting with his sister. Sita, now a helpless widow, under dire circumstances of poverty, has been compelled to prostitution and at her first night, she sees as her 'client' nobody else but her own brother.

The setting, that is, a rented room which has now turned into the 'ghar' (room) of a 'fresh girl', who has not done 'such things' before (as the landlady tells about Sita) becomes a bitter irony, undermining the idea of 'home'. It was in this very room that Abhiram and Sita sought to establish a household, with their child Binu. Ishwar stands unsteadily at the threshold of his sister's 'ghar' but before he can enter, Sita grabs a *bonti* (a kichen blade) and cuts her throat. The entire sequence, performing the self-immolation of Sita—a figure of mother, sister, wife—takes place inside the 'ghar'. The traditional domestication of woman and 'feminization' of the idea of 'home' get fragmented and blood-stained like the sacrificed body of Sita.

In the longest shot of the film, Ishwar and Sita, brother and sister look at each other. Ishwar cannot see her, because he is without his spectacles—both literally and metaphorically visionless. Sita's close-up, gazing at her brother, tragically reminds us of the 'Great Mother' archetype, which Ghatak repeatedly uses in his films. In *Subarnarekha* itself, an earlier shot shows that Sita was almost like a mother to her bachelor elder brother. Identities get "diffused, dissolved, dissipated" throughout the scene of Sita's suicide. Ishwar's face changes expressions: from a hopeless drunken man, carried away by the temptations of a city-night, he suddenly becomes a personification of lust, as his uncanny smile and blinking eyes tell us. The next moment, as Sita's blood gets sprinkled over his face, he appears to be wearing a white 'masque of death', with sweat all over his forehead and lips, as if suddenly a shocking epiphany has dawned on him.

The change of Ishwar's identity is evident: from his godlike, honest, idealistic and protective identity of an elder brother he is reduced to a morally decadent man who, later, like a figure of nemesis, cries out at the reporter, "You, me, all of us...are guilty. Do you think it's only my sister's tragedy? Don't you people have sisters?" This makes one realize how individual identities are always in a flux, and how the cultural identity of a Bengali family suffers from the epic crisis of partition and its subsequent blows on the society.

At the end of the film, Ishwar is on a return journey with his nephew Binu. The job and the company quarters must be vacated; Ishwar is once again homeless. But Binu, who has so often heard his mother Sita talk of their 'new home', now keeps asking his uncle about that 'home'. Ishwar walks along the bank of Subarnarekha, with the energetic and innocent Binu leading the way, in search of a 'new home'—which remains the only, however faint, 'golden line' of positive spirit in the film. This ceaseless search for a home and every refugee's struggle to cope up with a new identity is what comes with all the horror, hate, pain and yearning for a familiarity and foregone love.

After *Subarnarekha* (1962, released in 1965), Ghatak took a long gap before making *Titas Ekti Nodir Naam* (1973). *Titas* was produced in Bangladesh, released on 27 July 1973 in Dhaka, Narayanganj and Chittagong, and it was not until 1991 that the film could be shown in Kolkata. This instance of red-tapism itself seems to reflect the problem of rootlessness and identity. The greater Bengal's cultural identity, which was once like a vital stream (much as the river projected in the opening shot of the film), was threatened to lose its flow by the Partition, displacement and dissolution of communities (just as the river dries away in the movie). Throughout the film, the river is projected as its most important visual motif. Against a larger and vital flow, the drying banks around a small titular bend suggest that the flow is under the threat of getting lost some day. The visual motif not only suggests the drying up of the river's flow, but also foreshadows the tragedy of the East Bengali *Malo* fishing community, whose identity, life and sustenance depend upon the river.

The anxiety of losing one's 'home' and 'identity', as Ritwik Ghatak consciously shows, falls largely on young women to be married off: it is part of his larger thematic orientation towards the folk and the mythical that lies in the collective unconscious of the Bengali cultural identity. The scene with a closed door and an empty bed inside, implying the consummation of marriage between 'Rajar jhi' (daughter of Raja) and Kishore, depicts not only the usual anxiety surrounding a first sexual encounter, but the child bride's anguish of leaving her home and family. The situation of the child-bride carries a deeper allusion to the ritualistic custom of 'Gouridaan' at a very tender age. Gouri, conceptually the homely incarnation of Goddess Durga whom the Bengali culture had long accepted as a daughter-figure, is to be given away in marriage to the Shiva-like groom. The practice of 'Gouridaan' obviously affects the child-bride's psychology to a great extent: after this ritual she is no longer a part of her parents' home but somebody else's wife; in fear of falling into an unknown situation, alone with a man much older and little known, she has to travel far and struggle to make a new home in the in-law's house. The girl's pining for her parents and home before leaving it becomes evident in the shot where she falls at her mother's feet and starts weeping. And this scene functions as a premonition to the impending danger—the girl will soon be abducted from Kishore's boat, which in a broader sense, bears significance to the general ethos of rootlessness, lost identity and exile.

This abduction initiates a series of misery and suffering which makes both husband and wife victims of identity-crisis. The trauma of losing his bride turns Kishore insane, which again, may remind one of mythical allusions—Shiva's frenzied deeds after his separation from Sati, or, Ram's experience of loss and despair after the abduction of Sita. 'Rajar jhi', now separated from her home and husband, wanders across the country, along with a son presumably conceived during her first and only night spent with Kishore. Basanti, a young widow (who wanted to marry Kishore but was married to Subal, who also died) gives them shelter; and these two women set up a 'home' of sisterly bonding, without the presence of a man. A different idea of 'home' is established, only to be crushed afterwards, and thereby, reiterting the all-encompassing theme of rootlessness.

Ten years later, Kishore and 'Rajar jhi' meet under strange circumstances, and Kishore, now a madman recognizes her only for a brief moment, on the day of Doljatra (the Bengali version of Holi, the festival of colours). The moment is one of reclaiming identity, expressed through two opposite expressions and gestures on both sides. Kishore lifts 'Rajar jhi' and looks keenly at her face trying to recognize his lost wife, whereas she closes her eyes in a mode of submission; she has already felt the touch of her lost husband and no longer needs any confirmation. The consummation of their marriage, which, ten years back, made her so frightened and anxious of losing her 'virgin' identity, has now been a desirable moment of re-identification as a 'wife'—a moment of reunion which she awaits in silent submission to Kishore's arms. The moment is given a mythical flavour as the background score plays a folk song commemorating the union of Radha and Krishna. They have now found their 'home' not inside a bedchamber, but under the open sky, by the river. However, some village people notice them together and considering their relation adulterous, beat them severely. The two bodies left on the beach again make it clear how fragile the idea of 'home' is. With spasmic jerks, the woman tries to nurse her fatally injured husband with water, and he, before dying, can only utter one word—"Bou" (wife). Identity seems to be a like a ripple in the water, which takes shape and gets dissolved in a moment, as the sound of water lashing at the shore mingles with the gasps of the dying couple. Elsewhere Ghatak uses visual techniques to emphasize such moments of recognition and oblivion. In *Subarnarekha*, Abhiram through his writings, continues to search for his lost mother. And finally when he finds her, Kausalya cannot recognize him. Abhiram's face gets blurred against Kausalya's eyes.

Ghatak's films were more often than not, unsuccessful as far as the 'box office' was concerned. *Titas* was no exception; and perhaps, it received more negative criticisms than his other works. In one of his influential articles, Goutam Bhadra complains that Ghatak's film-version has failed to do justice to Advaita

Mallabarman's novel *Titas Ekti Nodir Naam*. According to him, Ghatak's urban middle class intellectual Bengali identity was far removed from the peripheral fishing community of the *Malo*s; from such a distance he could only romanticize their plight, by associating it with his typical and rather generalized nostalgia for the lost homeland during the Partition. The film emphasizes the relationships and rather ignores the social and economic plight of the *Malo* community. Bhadra argues: "In Ritwik's *Titas,* the Malo society seems to exist without its temporality, it has little association with the structures of economy at work in the larger world" (187, translation mine).

Ghatak, in fact, gave more importance to micro-histories which run parallel to the larger vision of economic and social changes, which seemed so problematic to a historian like Bhadra. The story of *Titas* does not end with the death of Kishore and 'Rajar jhi', it continues with their son Ananta and Basanti. The lonely and frustrated motherhood of Basanti sought to take care of the boy, but objections from her parents and feuds in the village compelled the boy to leave and find a 'home' elsewhere. On a wider level, many of the village people are also forced to leave their homes, in the face of threats projected by capitalistic encroachments upon their land. Basanti stays on to die alone. The river dries up at the end, and the *Malo* community gets dispersed and homeless, as the dried banks are occupied by an agricultural community. A mourning of loss and homelessness in general is thus rendered on screen, carrying a sense of lamentation for the extinction of a particular community.

The struggle for identity, the battle against the existential crisis can be found working at two levels in Ghatak's films. On the one hand, individuals fight for themselves, sometimes for the community, and sometimes, even abandoning the community. In Bengali culture, the meaning of 'home' covers a wide range of associations: house, family, land and also identity—both private and collective. In *Meghe Dhaka Tara*, Nita's sacrifice is meant for the maintenance of her *bari* or 'home', that is, in a larger sense, her family; while her mother keeps complaining that they will never be able to move to a large 'house'—a physical space viewed through a self-centred worldview. Haraprasad in

Subarnarekha neglects his family for the sake of his idealistic commitment to the community, and he can ultimately be of no use to anybody. *Titas Ekti Nodir Naam* also projects the *Malo* community's collective struggle for existence, but the characters lose the battle at the end—at both private and collective levels. In the last shot, against the dying agony of Basanti, we see a little boy running across the paddy fields, playing a 'bhnepu'. Whether we are to interpret it as a sign of hope is debatable; but this is at least clear that the child, still innocent, is free from the demands of life, living and identity yet to trouble his journey.

In Ritwik Ghatak's oeuvre, a mixture of traditional social and cultural insights with the pangs of modernity, alienation and loss of identity reflects the situation of post-Partition Bengal with all its hopes and desires, mourning and acceptance of defeat. However, the experience of homelessness and identity-crisis cannot be the same for every individual, and for the 'collective consciousnesses of every community. The pavement-dwellers in *Bari Theke Paliye*, the refugees in *Subarnarekha* and the *Malo*s in *Titas*—all experience the exile in their own ways, and finally, come to the bitter realization that dreaming of any kind of stable identity will ultimately lead to nowhere. Ghatak's 'identity' as an 'exilic' filmmaker paradoxically lies in his cinematic effort to render the ambiguity and fluidity of pre-partition Bengal's cultural memory and identity constantly being subject to interrogation and revision after the Independence.

Works Cited

Banerjee, Haimanti. *Ritwik Kumar Ghatak: A Monograph*. Pune: National Archive of India, 1985. Print.

Bari Theke Paliye. Directed by Ritwik Kumar Ghatak. L.B. Films International, 1958.

Bhadra, Gautam. "*Titas Ekti Nadir Naam*: Malor Chokhe". In *Ritwik Ghatak*. Ed. Rajat Ray. Kolkata: Srishti, 2001. Print.

Naficy, Hamid. *An Accented Cinema: Exilic and Diasporic Filmmaking*. Princeton: Princeton University Press, 2001. Print.

Subarna-rekha. Directed by Ritwik Kumar Ghatak. J.J. Films Corporation, 1962.

Titas Ekti Nodir Naam. Directed by Ritwik Kumar Ghatak. Purba Pran Kathachitra (Bangladesh), 1973.

12

Undesirable Aliens: Fissures of Nation, Polis and Self in *District 9*

Abin Chakraborty

Ziauddin Sardar reminds us that "Difference and otherness are the essence of aliens, for only then can they stiffen the sense of self and self-defence that completes the chain of science fiction as normative genre". Through the representation of aliens, in fact, science-fiction films either serve to consolidate those self-other binaries which often become the basis of military interventions, social discriminations or cultural triumphalism or strive to create a critical mirror that helps to interrogate some of the foundational divisions and prejudices governing our everyday lives. *District 9*, directed by Neill Blomkamp, belongs to the latter category as it interrogates entrenched hierarchies of segregation based on race, class and origin, that not only look back to the world of Apartheid-era South Africa but also the conflicts and controversies surrounding forcible evictions and relocation camps in today's world by focusing on the violent eviction of a group of migrant aliens settled in District 9 of Johannesburg, derogatorily identified as 'prawns'. In the process, the film piercingly challenges notions of compulsive homogeneity which often function as fundamental components of our sense of community and nation and the individual vehemence and institutional violence that are often applied to retain such homogeneity. Through the fate of Wikus Van der Merwe, an MNU official accidentally contaminated by alien DNA, who undergoes a gradual transformation, the film brings us face to face with the self/other binaries we regularly construct to fence off, from our cities, provinces or states all those we consider to be "undesirable aliens" and the dehumanizing consequences of such processes. The rest of the article would investigate in detail the nature of the multi-faceted political allegory which emerges in the process and analyze its relevance in the construction of identities and habitats, especially in postcolonial nations marked by heterogeneous communities and antagonistic histories.

The film revolves around the experiences of Wikus Van der Merwe, an employee of the Alien Affairs Department of Multi National United, a giant corporation which is also involved in a host of other businesses, including weapons manufacturing. Wikus is appointed as the head of an operation endorsed by the government to evict and re-settle the aliens located in the fenced and heavily militarized slum region, known as District 9, of an alternate Johannesburg where the film is set. The film informs us at the outset that these aliens were extricated from a malfunctioning large spaceship which came to be stranded over the city of Johannesburg in 1982, in a state of gross malnutrition, and placed within the area designated as District 9. However, while the initial settlement plans were based on the possibility of human-alien integration, the situation soon worsened, leading to riots, violence and casualties which culminated in a condition of massive public unrest regarding the very presence of the aliens and the demand to evict them from District 9. The process of eviction, however, leads to major confrontations between the aliens and the heavily armed mercenaries deployed by MNU, especially since there are obvious communicational barriers between the aliens and the humans and also because the aliens have very little understanding of the legal processes to which they are subjected. It is during this eviction drive, however, that Wikus is accidentally contaminated by alien DNA from a container that he was trying to confiscate. This begins a chain reaction where one of his arms begins to mutate into an alien organ along with associated physical alterations. But, instead of attempting to cure him in any way, the medical team at MNU only seeks to forcibly employ his alien organs for the successful testing of alien weapons and even conceal the truth of his condition from his wife. As Wikus escapes, the company even spawns propaganda about Wikus' contamination stemming from a supposed sexual liaison with aliens and he becomes an outcast and a criminal, rather than the unfortunate victim of an accident, deserving earnest medical attention. In desperation Wikus escapes to District 9 and forges an alliance with a couple of aliens attempting to re-start the alien mothership to return to their home planet in exchange of the possibility of securing a cure for himself. To succeed in their enterprise, they even break into the MNU headquarters to find the confiscated container, needed for re-starting the spaceship. This leads to an immediate escalation of the situation necessitating further deployment of heavily armed soldiers to hunt down Wikus and the aliens he had befriended. The final section of the film features extensive clashes between Wikus operating superior alien weaponry and MNU soldiers desperate to destroy him. Eventually, Wikus triumphs and his alien allies, a father-son duo, manage to restart the mothership and leave earth. Wikus disappears from official history and the film concludes with the acknowledgment of millions of aliens still stranded in District 10, the new settlement area to which they were being evicted. The conclusion does not offer any conclusive statement regarding the fate of these aliens or the possibility of any return of those who had escaped. We also remain unsure as to the fate of Wikus himself, even though the final shot seems to suggest that he has completely metamorphosed into an alien.

Through the development of this basic plotline, which capitalizes on the metaphoricity of aliens, the film explores on multiple levels the resonances associated with the term 'home' by weaving into the texture of the film considerations associated with race and class which govern the establishment and evolution of both nations and cities, the notions of selfhood on which such dynamics are premised and the ways in which the constructs of self, polis and nation are imbricated within the networks of multinational capital and the global tenets of techno-capitalist economy.

The thematic nub of the film of course revolves around human-alien conflict within the city of Johannesburg in relation to the alien settlement in District 9, with the aliens being addressed derogatorily as 'prawns' because of their physical features. The nomenclature of the both the aliens and their location within the city are endowed with obvious historical and political allusions. The name 'prawns' automatically evokes comparison with Hitler's consistent characterization of German Jews as pests, bugs, leeches and vermin who needed to be exterminated, as repeatedly mentioned in *Mein Kampf* (Hitler, 140, 157) and his speeches. The development of the subsequent idea of a German Fatherland of pure Aryan descent without the contaminating influence of the Jews was also congruent with those ideas of racial purity and attendant fears of miscegenation that have been at the heart of the politics of empire. As Aime Cesaire had pointed out, the Holocaust was in many ways a vengeful return to Europe of those very spectres that Europeans had unleashed in the colonies where thousands were exterminated because their humanity was denied on account of their skin colour (Cesaire, 36). The same paradigm was replayed with similar brutality in the segregation-ravaged American South or in the Apartheid era South Africa where African Americans or Black South Africans were subjected to horrible physical violence and systemic deprivations of many kinds. Whether for Hitler, the White Supremacists of the United States or the white rulers of Apartheid South Africa—the dehumanisation of Jews or non-white populations was based on an attempt to create a nation-space that included an exclusively racially homogeneous population. Such constructs function on the basis of an intersection of two mutually related ideas: the nation being a site of compulsive homogenization and the colonial world being governed by a Manichean logic (Fanon, 31) which keep the different races apart. So, just as the Nazis sought to annihilate the Jews or the European settlers in the American colonies massacred the aboriginal tribes (Ryan, 93-109; Gordon, 153-74), the employees of MNU and mercenaries hired by them think nothing of ruthlessly butchering the aliens in the name of either law and order or medical experiments or weapons testing. Particularly gruesome is the scene where an entire shack full of growing alien eggs is deliberately destroyed by fire by the MNU soldiers while Wikus exclaims how the exploding eggs sound like the preparation of popcorns.

Similarly, just as aboriginal tribes were forcibly evicted to different settlements in settler colonies like Australia, Canada or the United States, to separate them altogether from white populations (Atwood and Markus, 1999), in the same way, the aliens are being forcibly removed to a different settlement, District 10, to keep them as far apart as possible from the citizens of Johannesburg. Particularly telling is the scene where Wikus threatens to take away the son of an alien if it refuses to accept the eviction notice being handed to it. The scene alludes to the ways in which thousands of aboriginal children were separated from their families on the basis of colonial laws that conferred legal guardianship of all aboriginal children to the Chief Protector (Atwood and Markus, 8). The racial and colonial paradigms at work behind these operations are admitted by MNU employee Wikus Van der Merwe himself as he describes District 10 as being "more like a concentration camp". These associations are also bolstered by the historical fact of several violent and forcible removals which took place in post-Second World War South Africa where the Apartheid regime was responsible for the displacement of thousands of non-white people and the destruction of their residential localities. Based on the Group Areas Act of 1950, thousands of non-white people were evicted from their residences in Sophiatown in suburban Johannesburg, Cato Manor in Durban, District Six of Cape Town and several such other localities which were subsequently destroyed to make way for white residential areas (Abel, 3-8). As M. Legassick had previously pointed out,

> In the towns, all remnants of African land and property ownership have been removed, and a massive building programme of so-called 'locations' or 'townships' means that the African work force is housed in carefully segregated and police controlled areas that resemble mining compounds on a large scale. All the terms on which Africans could have the right to reside permanently in the towns have been whittled away so that today no African...has a right to permanent residence except in the 'reserves'. (qtd. in Wolpe, 63)

This is precisely the kind of systemic deprivation which District 9 foregrounds where we see that aliens are neither allowed to exist outside their settlement nor are they given access to the various urban facilities which citizens continually utilize. The unhygienic, insanitary and impoverished circumstances in which they are forced to live inside District 9 largely resemble the disheveled relocation camps or squatters' shacks where many evicted Africans had to take shelter during the apartheid regime. In the process, District 9 becomes a scathing indictment of the racist programmes of the Apartheid regime, evoked through a lens of defamiliarization designed to highlight the dehumanization which human beings can so callously mete out to fellow human beings on the basis of exclusionary narratives about self, home and nation. The same white supremacist ideology that led to the forcible evacuations of coloured Africans from various towns of the Union of South Africa thus finds its metaphoric equivalent in the confinement and eviction of aliens within and from District 9.

However, District 9 not only looks back to the past but also interrogates the present and the active fissures which continue to the haunt South African as well as Third World metropolises in general. The processes of urban gentrification are at work in both South Africa and other parts of the so-called developing world and as a result, cities are being spatially reconfigured in accordance with considerations of class which are leaving in their wake hundreds of people who are being forcibly evicted, relocated to areas marked by adverse living conditions and are being treated without the modicum of dignity and compassion which they as human being deserve. One might refer in this context to the eviction of the residents of the Joe Slovo informal settlement to temporary relocation areas in Delft as part of the N2 Gateway Project or the forced transportation of Symphony Way pavement dwellers to a temporary relocation area known as Blikkiesdorp which roughly translates as 'tin town'. A brief look at the following images would illustrate that there is significant similarity between places like Blikkiesdorp and the alien settlement portrayed in the film, where makeshift tents eventually gave way to ramshackle tin sheds. What is equally striking is the fact that these relocation areas experience the same kinds of impoverishment, insecurity and societal disintegration which one notices in life inside District 9 where gangs run rampant, scavenging is necessary for survival and the basic facilities of life are absent.

Such problems affect a large number of South African citizens as according to a report prepared by the Centre on Housing Rights and Evictions some 840000 people have been evicted within South African between 1995 and 2006 with around 5000 people being evicted in 2006 alone (COHRE 6). Such examples of postcolonial subalternization are associated with processes of gentrification through which more and more areas of the metropolitan cities, across the developing world, are being spatially reconfigured in such a way that the rich no longer have to tolerate the presence of a laboring underclass anywhere in their vicinity. So just as the processes of commodity fetishism drive the consumers away from the labour associated with their production to generate a seductive aura, in the same way, commercial residential estates often attribute to themselves a similarly hermetically sealed surrounding through processes of acquisition, eviction or compensation so that they become more desirable to potential consumers. At times, similar slum-eradication campaigns are carried out for the construction of modern transportation infrastructure, as was seen in the case of the Yamuna embankment slums, which were demolished on the basis of court orders to make way for metro rail, expressway and environmental conservation. Amnesty International therefore lamented that in the name of slum reductions "mass forced evictions are driving people further into poverty and thereby undermining all MDGs [Millennium Development Goals]"[1] and in one report, specifically declared that "Mass forced evictions of people living in slums are being carried out around the world, with Roma communities evicted across Europe, slum dwellers in Delhi forcibly evicted to make way for the Commonwealth Games and more than 200,000 people facing eviction in Port Harcourt, Nigeria". Widney Brown, Senior Director of International Law and Policy at Amnesty International, further stated that "From France to Zimbabwe to Cambodia, we have documented how governments are destroying homes of some of the poorest people in their countries. Those whose homes are destroyed are failed by the law, they get no compensation and no place to live."[2] These slum dwellers thus operate as the otherized beings of growing metropolises to whom we can conveniently deny human rights, the basic need for shelter and other amenities and that sense of dignity which we deem precious for ourselves. The way in which MNU officials serve eviction notices to the aliens, the way in which a mere touch of the papers is deemed is deemed informed acknowledgment, the brute force which is deployed, the way in which several aliens are arrested or killed—all symbolize this pervasive otherisation with which slum dwellers are often treated by governments and middle-class citizens. In the process, *District 9*, as a film, not only showcases the lines of segregation which constitute our cities, an extended version of 'home' but also the precariousness that underscores the homes of those who constitute the labouring underclass of the city.

Incidentally, the labouring underclass of various metropolitan cities is often formed by internal or external migrants who often survive through underpaid menial jobs even as the state refuses to legally sanction their existence and the society subjects them to ostracization. The starving, malnourished aliens whom the authorities choose to place in District 9 do resemble hordes of famished migrants and the tents that are arranged for them, along with aid workers and food supply, indeed resemble the visual imagery associated with newly established refugee camps with international funds in different border areas. Africa itself has been experiencing a great deal of refugee crisis, especially due to civil wars and protracted conflicts in several regions and the problem is equally true for various other countries in Asia, as well as different parts of Europe, in the wake of the recent refugee crisis. Much like the aborigines of the past and the poor of the present, the refugees of the present are often forced to live in camps and relocation camps in deplorable living conditions and also face a great deal of xenophobic hatred from native residents who often feel disgruntled by the state resources being used to maintain these camps, even as their various needs go unaddressed. The following lengthy description of the refugee settlement in Calais, rather aptly named 'the Jungle', which was demolished in 2016, provides a telling representation of the precariousness of refugee settlements in general:

> Situated on the outskirts of Calais, away from general view, the site of "the Jungle" is located next to two chemical plants. Here, migrants were forcibly moved by the authorities from a variety of smaller camps (or "Jungles") in 2015.... The hygienic conditions in "the Jungle" were rudimentary at best; one activist reports how she would step over "small rivers of human faeces from overflowing toilets" (Lewis Becoming, 21). The soil was difficult to keep out of tents, clothes, and even food. In cold weather conditions, fumes of burning plastic would fill the air, as people burned anything they could get their hands on to keep warm (*ibid*).... While state forces did next to nothing to improve the living conditions inside "the Jungle," the site was effectively turned into what has often been called a "caged Jungle," with fences, a wall paid for by the British government (Davies, Isakjee, and Dhesi 13), and a substantial police presence that would oftentimes hinder movement and subject refugees to unmotivated acts of both physical and verbal violence. (Koegler, 5)

Many of these features resemble life in District 9 and the physical similarity between the fictional site and actual refugee camps, such as the one in Calais, is also unmistakable.

Even more significantly, these refugee camps, as well as the alien settlement in *District 9*, may be said to function as those states of exception which far from signifying any temporary suspension of law become a "spatial arrangement that remains continually outside the normal state of law" (Mbembe 13). As a result, what one witnesses in these camps is a concatenation of disciplinary, biopolitical and necropolitical power in that the authorities have the power to impose regulations and punishments, subject the bodies of the migrants to indiscriminate checking, health hazards and physical torture and even kill them without compunction or judicial consequences. The same combination is witnessed in relation to the treatment of the aliens by the MNU officials and soldiers and the film therefore also becomes a representation of that necropolitics which divides human populations into those who are disposable and those who are not.

It is through the figure of Wikus Van der Merwe that both the aforementioned otherization and the precariousness become foregrounded. In fact, if home is also metaphorically associated with notions of selfhood and identity, then it is principally through the transformation of Wikus that these issues are explored. Initially, Wikus functions as the embodiment of the dominant perspective which is blatantly hateful of the aliens and treats them with utmost disgust, contempt and cruelty, especially in the scene where he destroys alien eggs and laughs as they explode. He freely abuses them, threatens them and considers them to be dangerous creatures which should be kept as far away from humans as possible. He thus acts as the representative of a particular type of selfhood which bases itself on those binaries of race and class that continue to foment systemic deprivations and atrocities just as they did in the past. However, once he becomes contaminated by alien DNA and begins to undergo physical transformation he finds himself on the receiving end of the dominant system and experiences first-hand the discrimination, humiliation and violence which he has so far meted out to the aliens. Furthermore, as he escapes from the MNU officials he is not only forced to seek shelter in the same District 9 which he once raided but is even compelled to live as a scavenger, much like the aliens themselves. Most importantly, once declared a fugitive, he comes under attack from the MNU mercenaries as well. What complicates matters further is that his own father-in-law is the one who betrays him and isolates him from his own family, especially his wife which subjects Wikus to great anguish. All of this also instils in Wikus a newfound sense of conscientious compassion as he establishes a new relationship with an alien father-son duo. Although the relationship is primarily a utilitarian one, based on Wikus' need to cure himself, it gradually evolves into something deeper and Wikus manages to continue assisting the aliens even when he realizes that he cannot be cured. He thus progresses towards a selfhood that no longer bases itself on foundational binaries of race, class or species which also entails more inclusive reconfigurations of the idea of home.

Such possibilities, however, remain quite distant in the film, especially since the workings of multinational capital, embodied by MNU, continue to consolidate those very hierarchies and exclusionary strategies which Wikus' predicament compels him to overcome. As the character of a sociologist named Sarah Livingstone informs us at the beginning of the film, MNU is the world's second largest weapons manufacturer and their involvement in the containment and transportation of aliens was primarily due to the urge to discover the mechanism of using alien weapons and sell them to the highest international bidder. The very reason why Wikus is treated as a guinea pig after his contamination is that his transformation enables him to fire the alien weapons in MNU's possession which had so far remained inoperable. The conclusion even informs us how the company was involved in illegal genetic research programmes. However, there is no reference to any action being taken against the company, even though Wikus' deputy Fundiswa is jailed for his role in exposing these illegal researches. We are also told how the entire District 9 settlement was demolished and the aliens shifted to District 10 which was inhabited by more than 2.5 million aliens and that it continues to grow. All of this suggests how the actions of the company are covertly or tacitly endorsed by the state which continues to follow the same policies of segregation and coercion that the rest of the film critiques. In the world of multinational capital, where virtually nothing escapes the entanglements of reification, life becomes a disposable object which might become the basis of further profit and the nation space becomes fissured accordingly.

Robert Scholes and Eric Rabkin had long ago described science fiction as "speculation and social criticism, hardware and exotic adventure" (38). *District 9* avoids exoticism but utilizes all the other aforementioned components to create a riveting examination of some of the foundational maladies associated with the colonialist and techno-capitalist discourse that continues to be normative in various parts of the world, especially in certain former colonies. Just as a classic is a cultural artefact that simultaneously works on several levels, District 9 too uses the aliens as a polysemic metaphor to examine intersecting issues of race, class, migration, gentrification, dehumanizing capitalist enterprises and much more to explore the different forms of unhomeliness and alienation that continue to haunt our everyday experiences. The aliens thus become the mirror through which humanity is sternly examined and found wanting.

Notes

https://www.amnesty.org/en/latest/news/2010/09/cumbre-odm-dirigentes-no-protegen-derechos-pobres/

https://www.amnesty.org/en/latest/news/2010/10/no-ignorar-mil-millones-habitantes-barrios-marginales/

Works Cited

Cesaire, Aime. *Discourse on Colonialism.* Trans. Joan Pinkham. Delhi: Aakar Books, 2010. Print.

District 9. Dir. Neill Blomkamp. Tristar Pictures, 2009.

Fanon, Frantz. *The Wretched of the Earth.* Trans. Constance Farrington. Harmondsworth: Penguin, 1969. Print.

Gordon, Michelle. "The Dynamics of British Colonial Violence". *Violence, Colonialism and Empire in the Modern World.* Eds. Phillip Dwyer and Amanda Nettlebeck. London: Palgrave Macmillan, 2018. Print.

Hitler, Adolf. *Mein Kampf.* Trans. James Murphy. London: Hurst and Blackett, 1939. Print.

Koegler, Caroline. "Precarious Urbanity: 'The Jungle' (Calais) and the Politics of Performing the Urban". *Postcolonial Text,* Vol. 12, Nos. 3 and 4 (2017). Print.

Mbembe, Achille. "Necropolitics". Trans. Libby Meintjes. *Public Culture,* 15.1 (2003). Print.

"MDG Summit: World Leaders Fail to Uphold Rights of the Poorest". Amnesty.org. 22 Sept. 2010. <https://www.amnesty.org/en/latest/news/2010/09/cumbre-odm-dirigentes-no-protegen-derechos-pobres/> Accessed on 17 Dec. 2017. Web.

Ryan, Lyndall. "Martial Law in the British Empire". *Violence, Colonialism and Empire in the Modern World.* Eds. Phillip Dwyer and Amanda Nettlebeck. Print.

Sardar, Ziauddin and Sean Cubitt. *Aliens R Us: The Other in Science Fiction Cinema*. London: Pluto Press, 2002. Print.

Scholes, Robert and Eric S. Rabkin. *Science Fiction: History, Science, Vision*. New York: Oxford University Press, 1977. Print.

"South Africa-Universal Period Review". Centre on housing Rights and Evictions. Geneva: Centre on Housing and Eviction Rights, 2008. <http://lib.ohchr.org/HRBodies/UPR/Documents/Session1/ZA/COHRE_ZAF_UPR_S1_2008_CentreonHousingRightsandEvictions_uprsubmission.pdf> Accessed on 17 Dec. 2017. Web.

Wolpe, Harold. "Capitalism and Cheap Labour Power in South Africa: From Segregation to Apartheid". *Segregation and Apartheid in Twentieth Century South Africa*. Eds. William Beinart and Saul Dubow. London: Routledge, 2003. Print.

"World Habitat Day: One billion slum dweller cannot be ignored". Amnesty.org. 01 Oct. 2010. <https://www.amnesty.org/en/latest/news/2010/10/no-ignorar-mil-millones-habitantes-barrios-marginales/> Accessed on 17 Dec. 2017. Web.

Reinventing Location: Texts in Search of a Home

13

From *Heart of Darkness* to *Apocalypse Now*: The Changing Face of Text-ness

Sagnik Banerjee

> My film is not a movie about Vietnam. It is Vietnam. It is what it was really like. It was crazy. And the way we made it was very much like the Americans were in Vietnam. We were in the jungle, there were too many of us. We had access to too much money and too much equipment and little by little, we went insane.[1] (Francis Ford Coppola)

In the press conference of the film's premier, this was how; filmmaker Francis Ford Coppola introduced his now magnum-opus war film, *Apocalypse Now* (1979) to the audience at the Cannes Film Festival.[2] A film, which is often referred to as a "flawed masterpiece, a magnificent failure" (Bogue, 611), or, as Roger Ebert, the noted film critic comments,

> "Apocalypse Now" is the best Vietnam film, one of the greatest of all films, because it pushes beyond the others, into the dark places of the soul. It is not about war so much as about how war reveals truths we would be happy never to discover. (Ebert, *Apocalypse Now*)

Coppola's film, is based on Joseph Conrad's novella *Heart of Darkness*, serialized in 1899 and published in 1902, is analogous to the narrative structure of *Heart of Darkness*. The original story sees the protagonist, Charlie Marlow, having secured a position with a Belgian company dealing in ivory trade in Africa, travelling up the Congo River, to locate and recall Kurtz, an agent of the company who has severed all ties with the company. "Upon arriving in Africa, Marlow finds that the company conducts its business with terrible cruelty toward its Congolese employees. He also finds that the competition for power among the company agents is ruthless and that Kurtz is widely resented by his colleagues for his alleged humanitarianism" (Matin, Introduction). Coppola's film is about Capt. Benjamin Willard, a US Army, Special Operations Officer, receiving a mission to travel up the Nung river into Cambodia to find and locate the renegade officer, Col. Walter E. Kurtz "who has become the god-king of a private army of Montagnards and U.S. deserters in Cambodia and who is waging war with the Americans and Viet Cong alike" (Bogue 613) and 'terminate his command' with 'extreme prejudice' (*Apocalypse Now Redux,* Original Screenplay)[3], and like his literary predecessor, Willard's journey through the hostilities, the visceral images of the Vietnam War that he witnesses and his final meeting with the 'enigmatic' Col. Kurtz, played by Marlon Brando, is a descent into the "heart of an immense darkness" (Conrad 95).[4]

The idea of a Vietnam War film was first put forward by the film's screenplay writer, John Milius and filmmaker George Lucas (Devine, Chap. 3) with the latter slated to direct the film. However, the idea was put forward to Coppola, who actually it can be said conceived of using Joseph Conrad's novella as the ethical and narrative framework to explore the extent of the moral and ethical dilapidation that the U.S. faced in their role as one of the important actors in the drama of this proxy-war being waged in Indochina. The path to adapting the text was by no means a simple one. Primarily among them was the very logistical difficulty of adapting or appropriating a Conrad text and secondly the failure to do so by one of his illustrious predecessor, namely Orson Welles, would have definitely been on Coppola's mind.[5] However, as Ronald L. Bogue comments, that the

> ...film should be viewed not as an adaptation, but an *imitation*—an imitation of Conrad's *Heart of Darkness*, just as Samuel Johnson's "Vanity of Human Wishes" is an imitation of Juvenal's Tenth Satire. (Bogue 612)

An exercise, he says, should not be viewed just as a timid exposition of substitution of the original text and neither is it a model of obeisance to an already existing structural framework, it is

> ...but a means of interrogating one's culture by juxtaposting it with an earlier culture. An imitation is a palimpsest: a manifest text constantly duplicating, displacing, correcting, and contradicting a latent text while insisting on its own autonomy...all convergences and divergences between the imitation and its model as significant statements about their relationship to one another. (*ibid.*)

This transformation from text to film and from one temporal and spatial matrix to another is one of the essential aspects in the understanding and the assessment of the text in the modern context, when the presence of a literary text per se, is by no means limited to the bound written word, but the multifarious possibilities that open up the rendition and reception of a text, to the level where the very location of the 'text' can be questioned by the palimpsest nature of adaptation itself; the text can be verifiably said to have migrated. Through this paper, I plan to re-read Conrad's novella *Heart of Darkness* (1899) paralleled with Francis Ford Coppola's *Apocalypse Now* (1979) and trace the contours of the changing face of text-ness and chart the course of the textual migration through the literary, cinematic and cultural topographies across time, assessing the evolution of Conrad's novella into Coppola's film, temporally, spatially and contextually trying to find the location of the text, or assess whether the text actually inhabits in a 'non-place'.

The adaptation of the literary to the cinematic is one of the most prevalent textual transformations observable, since the advent of the cinematic art as one of the fundamentally important art forms in the 20th century. By Conrad's own admission, he speaks of his task, or what hc is trying to achieve "by the power of the written word, to make you hear, to make you feel—it is, above all, to make you see" (*The Nigger of the Narcissus* vii), is emblematic of the "cinematic qualities of his pre-Modernist writings" (Sherry, 374). After the advent of cinema as a popular art form into mainstream culture, "the importance of film as a means of transmitting influence should not be underestimated" and also in the case of the dissemination of Conrad's text into mainstream culture, the importance of cinematic appropriations become a focal point of study, especially when "far more people will have seen film versions of Conrad's works than have actually read his books" (Moore, 236), thereby opening up the possibilities of multiple interpretations and cultural appropriations which an otherwise literary text would not have endured. Before we analyse the nature of such a migration, we must first assess the nature of textual migration itself.

The first question that arises is what is migration? A Google search of the word's definition, yields three results, the first outlines it as a seasonal movement of animals from one region to another, the second calls it as a movement of people to new area or country in order to find work or better living conditions, and the third as a movement from one part of something to another. If we eliminate the third possibility as being essential of the inanimate objects, the remaining two observations brings in two possibilities, (a) either migration is natural, that is being a cyclic movement in the course of time and repetitive in nature, as akin to the avian family, and (b) where there exists, a pre-condition ('in order to') for migration. Migration occurs sometimes by choice, or by instinct or by compulsion. It is a movement, but unlike others, it is a movement "across geographical, national and/or cultural boundaries or differences" (Janz, 287). One of the fundamental aspects then of migration is that migration almost at all levels entails an adaptation. "We rarely speak of someone or something as having migrated if no change or adaptation was required" (*ibid.*). The nature of migration brings in essential issues of time and place. Bruce Janz refers to Deleuze and Guattari, who in their essay[6] speaks of the nomad, the people or animals who "do not move to a dwelling but dwell by moving" (*ibid.*), in essence speaking of the rhizomatic nature of their existence, always adaptive and are defined by their movement and their current environment. Also, the question of 'Home' bears an important consideration in the question of migration. What can be defined as home? Is it the existence, prior to migration, or post-migration, the 'new' space that becomes home? The transformation of home from a lived 'space' to one that in Rushdie's terms can be referred to as imaginary homelands. But what is exactly meant, when we refer to the migration of a text? William Sweet, in his introduction to the seminal work *Migrating Texts and Traditions* (2012) outlines,

> By 'migration' here we mean that the text or tradition has come to, has taken root in and developed, and perhaps sometimes has even flourished in an environment that is far from its origin, and yet there is also a continuity and consistency—and (with texts) a univocity—with that origin. (Sweet, 2)

One of the first understandings that needs to be ascertained is that, in case of textual migration, despite the fact that when a literary text migrates, it essentially gets stripped of its fundamental identical markers and the change occurs to meet the textual demands of specific geo-political and temporal space into which the text is migrating; however, both the texts, separated by historical and geographical spaces share an essential continuous core and it is that which entailed the adaptation in the first place.

Assessing *Apocalypse Now* as the hypertext of Conrad's *Heart of Darkness* (in this case the hypotext), borne out of the height of 19th century European colonialism and transformed into the neo-colonial situation exhibited during the 20th century, with the Vietnam War as the ever present motif is an important aspect of consideration indeed. The textual identity of Conrad's novella gets re-appropriated, from a text born out of the frailty of the 'white man's enterprise' in Africa to the massive failures of the American efforts in Vietnam. Both Marlow and Willard's journeys in their core entail a journey into the deepest paradoxes of the self.

One of the first aspects of consideration in the journey that the text takes is to trace its transformation across medium, from a literary text to a cinematic one. Conrad's novel published in 1902, in the height of the pre-modernist tradition, something which would inspire later authors like Virginia Woolf and

T.S. Eliot.[7] As stated earlier, one of his primary literary attributes was directed towards the visual aspect of his novel, making them essentially 'picturesque', and of the inherent cinematic qualities in his writings. However if we are to consider this transformation, one of the important aspects to bear in mind would be the socio-historical development of film as a medium, and mostly cinema as an industry and the economic and political implications of it. *Apocalypse Now*, with Michael Cimino's *The Deer Hunter* (1978) arrived in consecutive years as documents of America's bruised psyche due to the conflict in Vietnam. And Coppola's film, with the later *Apocalypse Now Redux* (2011), as adaptation of *Heart of Darkness* has transformed the critical approaches to the novel (Sherry, 374). The industrial structure of film as an art form, has radically altered the author-text relationship and more than ever, the cinematic hypertext is not just a palimpsest bearing traces of the source hypotext, but also by nature of the medium, exposed to multifarious factors which affect the nature of the transformation, transition and eventual migration of the text into its current form.

Though, cinematically evocative, *Heart of Darkness* opens up logistical difficulties for any filmmaker owing to location, expenses and a narrative ambiguity, which demands experimental modes of filming, which at times popular studio houses refuse to support, as Orson Welles, discovered in 1939. In Coppola's case, the very fact that the film actually got made, was partly due to the massive influence the new auteurs had in Hollywood, and especially after the successes of his *Godfather I and II*, Coppola himself had. Coppola adapted Conrad's tale of colonial exploitation, in and as "an adventure/mystery tale through the specific conventions of the hard-boiled detective formula" (Hellmann, 57). Marlow's transformation into Willard is from an ivory agent, to that of an assassin, though both are connected to the core theme of exploitation. And whereas Marlow essentially is emblematic of the white man in Africa, Willard is part of the neo-colonial capitalist forces of the US Army. Coppola's film, while adapting *Heart of Darkness* becomes part of the literary tradition of Conrad, and is influenced by it with his own cinematic medium, its history also acting as a frame of reference, to the point that Conrad's text gets in effect re-appropriated. Willard in *Apocalypse Now*, reminiscences the urban detective character and even his voice-over narration[8] with its ironies, the similes and essential laid back nature, bears the elements of the detective trope, though vaguely, with "overtones of pulp literature and comic books" (Hellmann, 68). John Hellmann traces the similarities between the two texts,

> There are important similarities, reflecting their common source in quest myths, between *Heart of Darkness* and the hard-boiled detective formula. Both have isolated protagonists on a mystery/adventure who are in the employ of others while actually preserving their personal autonomy of judgment. In both works the protagonists encounters revelatory scenes of depravity of his society in the course of his journey. And the final apprehension of the 'criminal' (my quotes), while on the surface restoring moral order, actually ends in dissolution, with the protagonist more cynical about his world than before. (Hellmann, 69)

Hence, a Marlow, comments how, "The conquest of the earth, which mostly means the taking it away from those who have a different complexion or slightly flatter noses than ourselves, is not a pretty thing when you look into it too much" (Conrad 21) and his disgust at "the philanthropic pretence of the whole concern" (Conrad 39) and Willard comments after the shooting episode on the boat, "It was a way we had over here of living with ourselves. We'd cut them in half with a machine gun, and give them a Band-Aid". Marlow's character and his journey gets re-appropriated in the hands of Coppola to the metaphorical detective of the Hollywood tradition, at the same time is a commentator on the cultural depravity that was witnessed on and during the Vietnam War, and in general America's involvement in the East, which in turn acts as a visual metaphor to the journey of Charlie Marlow in Conrad's novel.

The film itself, as a text, mirrors the very journey it portrays and adapts, and hence opens its interpretative and adaptive apparatuses to various para-textual influences which act not only as markers for Coppola's film, but also a cultural and political presentation in contemporary times but also influences the reading of Conrad's novella. The reception of the film has been guided by its well publicized and infamous production troubles, vividly portrayed in Eleanor Coppola's documentary *Hearts of Darkness: A Filmmaker's Apocalypse* (1991) and her *Notes on the Making of Apocalypse Now* (1991). "These paratexts add another complex layer of intertextual interruption-informing and amending the discourse between reader and Conrad's precursor novella" (Sherry, 375) and act as important focal points in tracing the journey of the text, from Conrad to Coppola and eventually to the reader/audience.

A film, as a production phenomenon, opens itself up to limitless possibilities in the form of paratextual materials. As Eleanor Coppola's documentary notes, the horrid nature and conditions of filming *Apocalypse Now*, is in some way reminiscent of the problems the European 'white man' faced while 'civilizing' the African terrain. Coppola's film crew experienced the same hostile situations, landscape as Marlow's contemporaries would have faced in Congo. "If the production of a film can mirror the narrative of the fictional story being made, then *Hearts of Darkness: A Filmmaker's Apocalypse* stands as the apex of this mutuality" (Sherry, 386). The documentary capturing the filming of *Apocalypse Now* serving inadvertently a visual and cinematic reminder of the realities of the source, of its source text, as the crew battles, typhoons where part of the sets were dismantled, Harvey Keitel being cast as Willard, only later replaced by Martin Sheen weeks into the shooting with Sheen himself suffering a heart-attack, an over spiralling budget,[9] long drawn shooting schedule and even Marlon Brando being overweight; all forced technical and creative challenges to the making of the film. The film itself becomes a metaphor of an American cultural intrusion into the proverbial darkness of Vietnam, mirror in some way the ethos explained by Marlow in Conrad's novella,

> I came upon a boiler wallowing in the grass, then found a path leading up the hill. It turned aside for the boulders, and also for an undersized railway truck lying there on

> its back with its wheels in the air. One was off. The thing looked as dead as the carcass of some animal. I came upon more pieces of decaying machinery, a stack of rusty rails. (Conrad, 30)

Eleanor's diary, notes Jamie Sherry, "describes the lavish circumstances that they enjoyed filming in Manila. It describes decadence, the colonial need to replicate the pleasures of home" and he notes how Coppola becomes a rendition of a modern day Kurtz (Sherry, 387), with the film itself being his own journey into the proverbial heart of darkness.

The relationship between Coppola's film, Conrad's text and the external realities manifest in the filmmaking process, both historical and socio-political situations play their part as the interpretative apparatus and transform the reception of both texts and bear important influences in the journey from Conrad to Coppola. With the film, Coppola tries to capture "a sense of the horror, the madness, the sensuousness of the Vietnam war" (Kinder, 13) as explained by the filmmaker himself in his promotional brochure which was distributed at the theatre. However, much like Conrad's Kurtz, the massive televized madness and the powerful impact of the war which affected American consciousness prompted Coppola to explore to the limit, much to the dismay of his own wife, who felt that her husband was "creating the very situation he went there to expose" (Coppola, 159).

One of the fundamental markers in locating the journey from *Heart of Darkness* to *Apocalypse Now* as texts, and which in turn act as interpretative influences is the character of Kurtz himself, the only character who remain unchanged in name in Coppola's film. Mainstream culture sees Brando's rendition as emblematic of Conrad's Kurtz and in Eleanor Coppola's documentary, we see Brando admitting, not having read *Heart of Darkness* or any of the drafts of the screenplay of the film. In a way he was re-interpreting the character from Orson Welles' *Citizen Kane*, inhabiting a proverbial wasteland, where he recites Eliot, and has James Fraser's *The Golden Bough* (1890) and Jessie L. Weston's *From Ritual to Romance* (1920) in his personal collection in the jungle; two books which acted as primary influences on T.S. Eliot while writing his magnum opus *The Waste Land* (1921). Kurtz's adaptation as a mythic, almost larger than life figure, a sort of psychological 'shadow' for Willard, opens the journey to a multitude of influences both cinematic and literal, where Brando's character is influenced by both Conrad's interpretation and Welles' Kane and culturally all the three figures mutually co-exist in the interpretative paradigms effecting both Conrad's novella and Coppola's film.

Apocalypse Now's relation to its source text, and any assessment of the trajectory of the journey between the two, would be incomplete if the film itself is not placed historically within the tradition of its precursor cinematic texts. Amongst them, other than Welles' failed attempt at adapting Conrad's text to film, there are Werner Herzog's *Aguirre, the Wrath of God* (1972) another psychological exploration based on a river journey into the heart of the Amazonian forest, and Michael Herr's *Dispatches* (1977), a collection of reminiscences from Vietnam veterans. Though not officially mentioned, the influence of Conrad's novella on the film is expressed in his own words, noted in the printed screenplay of the film. Sherry quotes,

> Instead of carrying the script day-to-day, I had a little green paperback of Conrad's *Heart of Darkness* in my pocket, filled with notes and markings. I just naturally started referring to it more than the script, and step by step, the film became more surreal and reminiscent of the great Conrad novella. (Sherry, 377)

The very question of locating the two texts, within two time frames and their contextual journey is perhaps one of the most fundamentally essential aspects that mark this migration. Not just, the literary and cinematic precursors that frame Conrad and Coppola's texts, both essentially located in history and both mutually interpreting/creating a combined textual experience, where in mainstream culture *Apocalypse Now* becomes an audio-visual transformation of the context of Conrad's novel. Whereas Conrad's novel loosely explore the colonial exploitation of Congo, where King Leopold's agents from Belgium under humanitarian pretences converted the country into a forced labour camp for extraction of ivory and later during the 1890's, rubber (Matin, Introduction). In addition to outright murders the horrific conditions that resulted as a product of imperial expansionist politics in the region. The sheer humanitarian crisis and imperial carnage can be estimated with the death toll ranging in the millions, coupled with starvation, disease and a steeply declining birth-rate, a reality noted by Marlow, who observes the condition of the indigenous workers,

> Six black men advanced in a file, toiling up the path. They walked erect and slow, balancing small baskets full of earth on their heads.... Black rags were would round their loins, and the short ends behind waggled to and fro like tails. (Conrad, 30)

Something which reminiscences scenes from Dante's *Inferno*, (Matin, Introduction), Marlow notes,

> Black shapes crouched, lay, sat between the trees, leaning against the trunks, clinging to the earth, half coming out, half effaced within the dim light, in all the attitudes of pain, abandonment and despair...this was the place where some of the helpers had withdrawn to die. (Conrad, 31-32)

Marlow's reference to the native workers as "nothing but black shadows of disease and starvation, lying confusedly in the greenish gloom" (Conrad, 32) actually is carried as a visual reminiscence in many of the surreal visual sequences in Coppola's film.

The obvious transposition of colonialism in Conrad with the Vietnam War in Coppola would be a simplistic way of looking at the transformation of the text, and perhaps a one-dimensional way of looking at them. Conrad's novel is as much about the effects of the colonial enterprise, the innate hollowness of the exercise as Coppola's film is about the hollowness of the American involvement in the War. However, "War is much more the subject of his film than is colonialism the subject of Conrad's novel" (Bogue, 614). The similarity in both the enterprises is striking. Conrad's novel is essentially about the capitalist exploitation for the European market, with colonialism having direct lineage to economic expansion of Europe, and in

Coppola when we see Brando's Kurtz telling Willard, that he is neither an assassin nor a soldier, but "an errand boy for grocery clerks come to collect the price" (*Apocalypse Now Redux*, Screenplay), he is referring to the unmistakable capitalist strain of the whole endeavour in Vietnam, attempted to stop the progress of communism in the region, and in a way localizing the text. Colonialism and explorations of colonialism were perhaps never the primary concern of Conrad, and though he doesn't approve it, he sees it as a necessary strain in the endeavour of human existence, "[T]he price of civilization, it would seem is the barbarity of colonialism" (*ibid.*). Coppola does not place his film in the larger context of America's expansionist politics, but instead localizes it. It can be said that this is perhaps due to the visual aspect of the cinematic medium on one hand as well as the influence of contemporary politics on the American psyche on the other, and both of them co-opting to create a visually intense experience. Cinema as a medium always requires focusing on the particular, with the camera being the eye through which the narrative is explored, hence the migration entailed the journey within the novel, the very act of 'seeing' occupy a primacy of experience. And in that localization, the 'sepulchral city' of Conrad is not some far off land from which the lone white man traverses an Odyssean space venturing into unknown territory, but the imperialist culture, is now part of the colonized space. In Coppola, the 'sepulchral city' is not Washington DC, but Saigon itself.

Coppola was keen to explore the madness of the war in Vietnam, and he does so through episodes and characters. Whether be it a young seventeen year old soldier, Clean murdering out of nervousness, an entire Vietnamese family, or be it the various difficulties and guerrilla attacks faced by the PBR in its journey up river, or through the character of Col. Kilgore, who is a "caricature of the military mentality" (Bogue, 615) in Vietnam, who comments in one of the movie's famous dialogues, "I love the smell of napalm in the morning... [it] smelled like victory". Colonialism, vis-a-vis the Vietnam conflict, occupies a much more central concern in Coppola than it does in Conrad. "Colonialism interests Conrad because the colonizer in his confrontation with savages and the lawless jungle faces the primeval essence of his being" (Bogue, 614), whereas, the 'savagery' in Coppola is directly ascertained to the horrors of war, the inherent madness affecting both the US soldiers and Viet-Cong alike. In the film Kurtz speaks about how the Viet-Cong, hacked off arms off every children of a village which had been inoculated for polio by the Special Forces of the US military, and the incident (though not historically verified), gives Kurtz, the fundamental truth regarding the conflict, "And then I realized, they were stronger than we. Because they could stand it.... You have to have men who are moral, and at the same time, who are able to utilize their primordial instincts to kill without feeling, without passion. Without judgment. Without Judgment. Because it's judgment that defeats us...". This in essence was the moral implication of the war, the neo-colonial political reality which Coppola as an artist and cinematic auteur sought to explore.

The central image of the novel gets appropriated in the film, that of the river and the journey up-river. Marlow refers to Congo as "an immense snake uncoiled" that "fascinated me as a snake would a bird" (Conrad, 22) and that "Going up that river was like travelling back to the earliest beginnings of the world" (Conrad, 49). The film too is motivated by the structure of the journey up the Nung River, "that snaked through the war like a main circuit cable", and which carries Willard to Cambodia towards Kurtz. The journey of the central character mirrors the journey that the two texts themselves take in time and space, reinventing each other. Marlow's journey as a voyage through time to the primitive past of man bears a transformation in Willard's journey. In essence, he is not going back to the past, but a journey into the hearts of the consciousness of which the conflict is a large part.

One of the primary considerations when locating a text, or tracing its migration, is the consideration of the recipient. A text, with its multiple influences operates on the plane of the reader/audience's cognition. For the modern reader, the tropes of cultural consumption and the capitalist, industrial nature of the cinematic medium itself, render visual motifs as extremely essential cultural artefacts. The Vietnam conflict and its excesses have been adapted cinematically in a multitude of Hollywood productions, where the basic nature of the neo-colonial reality becomes a redundant paratextual excess to the actual visceral imagery of war: the implications of the images in the consciousness of the post-modern individual. Technological advancements in the vastly changing modern world, with re-mapped geo-political boundaries, have changed all perspectives. There are many who find a parallel between the colonial enterprise in Conrad and the modern American foreign policy. Culturally, the savagery in Conrad finds its re-appropriation, ironically not in the Montagnards guarding Kurtz, but in the American presence itself which provides ample opportunities for the expression of savage passions. In a conflict, time and space where the manic nature of the time gets re-enhanced, Kurtz sought control over the senselessness by becoming a renegade and being a 'god' to the Montagnards. When Kurtz asks Willard, whether his methods are unsound or not, Willard's statement inadvertently exposes the nature of the American presence as expressed in the film, "I don't see any method at all Sir".

The textual migration from literary to the cinematic, explored in this paper, entails us to look into further questions, like the cultural and linguistic specificity of texts. Can a text actually migrate? Texts, it is argued are deeply culture specific and are bearers of the mark of specific cultural and temporal space in which they originate. Some argue that texts may migrate into alien traditions, but bear similar structures and philosophical questions. Relating these challenges, to the textual migration discussed specifically in this paper, one can definitely argue that, the possibilities of migration of texts, and especially literary texts are endless, as adaptations into multiple mediums and cultures. Migrations occur across time as well, both linguistically and culturally. Translations essentially entail the spirit of textual migrations as well. However, one has to note the fact of the essential core of the hypotext and the hypertext bearing a close resemblance, though there may be a new effort at identity formation, which "may well have a history and even a politics" (Janz, 294) rendering newer politics of space and rendition to the text.

Heart of Darkness's migration to Coppola's war epic *Apocalypse Now* is a cultural reference point, where temporality and spatiality converge to create a unique space for the location of the text. Both Conrad's novella and Coppola's film it might be argued are located in their geo-temporal and political specificities. However, it also needs to be acknowledged that any reading of the text, in the contemporary frame of reference, cannot exclude the cultural psyche that has created the images of the Vietnam Conflict, and even much later, the Iraq War (2003-11), and the human rights violations at Abu Gharib Prison. The film in a way has rendered Conrad's text culturally and politically relevant to readers in a technological society for whom, a journey up an African river does not portray the darkness of man, but rather it is the journey within, and it is this inward journey that forms the core of both the narrative structures, and it is there that we must locate Conrad's novella and Coppola's film.

Notes

1. Quoted from the Google Books version of *Vietnam at 24 Frames a Second: A Critical and Thematic Analysis of over 400 Films about the Vietnam War* by Jeremy M. Devine. p. 185.
2. The film went on to win the coveted *Palme D'Or* or the highest honour at the Film Festival in 1979, where it was tied with Volker Schlondorff's *Die Blechtrommel* (The Tin Drum), another adaptation of the Gunter Grass novel of the same name.
3. All quotations from the film are from the original screenplay of *Apocalypse Now Redux*, by John Milius and Francis Ford Coppola with narration by Michael Herr procured from the website, *www. dailyscript.com* <http://www.dailyscript.com/scripts/apocalypsenowredux.html>.
4. All textual references to *Heart of Darkness* would be from this book.
5. Orson Welles in 1939 planned an experimental adaptation of *Heart of Darkness*, which was unsuccessful. Welles eventually had to abandon the idea with "RKO studios turning their back on a prohibitively expensive production" (Sherry 380). He would later go on to film *Citizen Kane* as his debut feature, which too was an examination of "the fall of a powerful and influential man who has embarked on a corrupting, self-destructive path" (*ibid.*).

6. Deleuze Gilles and Felix Guattari, *A Thousand Plateaus: Capitalism and Schizophrenia*. Trans. Brian Massumi. Minneapolis: University of Minnesota Press, 1987. Print.
7. Eliot used the concise assertion, "Mistah Kurtz—he dead." as the epigraph of his poem "The Hollow Men" (1925) and even planned to use the passage from *Heart of Darkness*, that ended with Kurtz' famous death remark, "The horror! The horror!" until he was persuaded otherwise by Ezra Pound.
8. Michael Herr who wrote the evocative *Dispatches*, as a commentary on the war, wrote the narrations of Willard.
9. Coppola critiques his own work in his wife's documentary, including admitting that his film "is a $20 million disaster, why won't anyone believe me? I'm thinking of shooting myself" (Sherry, 386).

Works Cited

Apocalypse Now. Dir. Francis Ford Coppola. Screenplay by John Milius and Francis Ford Coppola. Perf. Martin Sheen, Marlon Brando, Robert Duvall. Zoetrope, 1979. Film.

Bogue, Ronald L. "The Heartless Darkness of "Apocalypse Now."" *The Georgia Review*, 35.3 (1981): 611-26. *JSTOR*. Web. 25 Sep. 2015.

Conrad, Joseph. *Heart of Darkness*. ed. Ross C. 2nd ed. Boston: Murfin. Palgrave Macmillan, Bedford Books, 1996. Print.

———. *The Nigger of Narcissus*. 1897. ed. John Berseth. New York: Mineola, Dover Publication, 1999. *Google Book Search*. Web. 12 Oct. 2017.

Coppola, E. *Notes on the Making of Apocalypse Now*. London: Faber & Faber, 1991. Print.

Devine, Jeremy M. *Vietnam at 24 Frames a Second: A Critical and Thematic Analysis of over 400 Films about the Vietnam War*. Austin: University of Texas Press, 1995, 1999. *Google Book Search*. Web. 7 Oct. 2017.

Ebert, Roger. "Apocalypse Now, Review" *www.rogerebert.com*. Roger Ebert, 28 Nov. 1999. Web. 10 Oct. 2017. <http://www.rogerebert.com/reviews/great-movie-apocalypse-now-1979>

Hearts of Darkness: A Filmmaker's Apocalypse. Dir. F. Bahr, G. Hickenlooper and E. Coppola. USA: Paramount, 1991. Film.

Hellmann, John. "Vietnam and the Hollywood Genre Film: Inversions of American Mythology in *The Deer Hunter* and *Apocalypse*

Now". *Inventing Vietnam: The War in Film and Television*. Ed. Michael Andregg. Philadelphia: Temple University Press, 1991. Print. Culture and the Moving Image.

Janz, Bruce. "Philosophy-in-Place and Texts Out of Place". *Migrating Texts and Traditions*. Ed. William Sweet. Ottawa: University of Ottawa Press, 2012. *Google Book Search*. Web. 11 Oct. 2017.

Kinder, Marsha. "The Power of Adaptation in Apocalypse Now." *Film Quarterly*, 33.2 (1979-1980): 12-20. *JSTOR*. Web. 4 Oct. 2017.

Matin, A. Michael. "Introduction", *Heart of Darkness and Selected Short Fiction*. New York: Barnes and Noble Inc., 2003. epub Edition.

Milius, John and Francis Ford Coppola. *Apocalypse Now Redux: Original Screenplay*. n.pag. n.d. Web. 10 Oct. 2017.

Moore, Gene M. "Conrad's Influence". *The Cambridge Companion to Joseph Conrad*. Ed. J.H. Stape. Cambridge: Cambridge University Press, 1996, 223-40. Print.

Sherry, Jamie. "Paratextual Adaptation: *Heart of Darkness* as *Heart of Darkness* via *Apocalypse Now*". *A Companion to Literature, Film and Adaptation*. Ed. Deborah Cartmell. London: Wiley-Blackwell, 2012. Print.

Sweet, Michael. "What does it Mean for Texts and Traditions to Migrate?" *Migrating Texts and Traditions*. Ed. William Sweet. Ottawa: University of Ottawa Press, 2012. *Google Book Search*. Web. 11 Oct. 2017.

14

Comics Journalism and the Question of Authenticity: A Reading of Joe Sacco's *Safe Area Goražde*

Saikat Sarkar

During his *Yahoo* phase the Maltese American comic artist Joe Sacco published an intriguing autobiographical short work of graphic narrative named "How I Loved the War" (published later in the volume, *Notes from a Defeatist*). This was 1991, a time when Sacco was living in Berlin and was deeply moved by the Gulf War, a time before he published works like *Palestine* (2001) and *Safe Area Goražde: The War in Eastern Bosnia 1992-1995* (2000) which would make him famous worldwide. This was a time when a young Sacco was having problems maintaining a long-distance relationship with his girlfriend. The world outside was engaged with the Gulf War and Sacco was interested in the nature of the media coverage of the war. And then there was his classmate from a German language learning course, Ali, a man originally from Palestine. There is one striking page in "How I loved the War" comprising of three panels; two small ones on top and a large one at the bottom. In the two smaller panels the narrative focuses on Sacco lying on the bed trying to connect with her girlfriend over phone and switching on the TV set to connect to other people's pain. But the pain, occasioned by the raging Gulf War, is too enormous and distant for Sacco to feel. In the lower panel, we see Ali's grimaced face against a confined landscape lined with dark houses. Around the face there are small narratives telling us the jarring life-story of Ali "whose family fled Palestine in the 1948 fighting...whose house in Beirut was destroyed in the Lebanese Civil War...whose grandfather's brother was massacred at Shatila during Israel's 'Peace for Galilee' invasion" (188). The whole panel has only Ali with Sacco lying outside the frame. But he is inside the frame too asking Ali questions, asking what he thought about the war. Ali's words, marked in the solitary speech balloon, are short and poignant. "You cannot imagine how I feel" (188) replies Ali. These few words cogently bring to us a range of aspects which imbricate into each other: Ali's experience of devastation; his feeling of homelessness; and Sacco's realization that he indeed couldn't imagine. These panels, telling in their effect, make us aware of the different dimensions of Sacco's work. One major area that Sacco's work is concerned with is the question of authenticity of representation, who can authentically relate and who can speak for himself. This question becomes all the more loaded with implications when one realizes that for Sacco the question is additionally linked to his medium of expression, of what he calls comics journalism. Ali's striking words draw light to another significant aspect of the subjects Sacco deals with; the issue of homelessness, an issue which has become highly pertinent in today's world besotted with wars and migrations.

In his now well-known "Introduction" to Joe Sacco's *Palestine*, Edward Said has noted the general tone of aspersion that adult readers of literature feel vis-à-vis comic books. Going against this usual grain of reading, in the same "Introduction", Said observes how insightfully Sacco captures the essence of Intifada in this visual narrative and how the art of this "unusual portrayer of life...has the power to detain us" (v). Comic or graphic narratives of fiction have traveled a long way from being a 'tier' of 'panels' with 'gutters' in between in the newspapers to be developed as elaborately designed narratives in 'panels' that is equivalent in form and dimensions to the prose novel. Though the artists of these narratives, such as Joe Sacco, refuse the label of graphic novel as something of a marketing strategy the term graphic novel is now accepted as a visual narrative which is greater than a comic book in its ambition. Graphic novel is a new genre in formation and is still in the process of unmaking and remaking itself.

Expectedly the anxiety to prove the legitimacy of the genre is unmistakable among the writers and readers of graphic narratives. Talking about the truthfulness of Sacco's presentation of reality Said, grading the narrative in terms of novels and poems, opines that with "the exception of one or two novelists and poets, no one has ever rendered this terrible state of affairs better than Joe Sacco" (iii). Such comparisons are inevitable as graphic narratives have developed from comics, a genre thought by many to be fitting for children only. Said's opening words of his "Introduction" to *Palestine* underscore the general feeling:

> Comic books are a universal phenomenon associated with adolescence. They seem to exist in all languages and cultures, from East to West. In subject matter they go the whole range from inspired and fantastic to sentimental and silly; all of them, however, are easy to read, to pass around, store, and throw away.... Most adults, I think, tend to connect comics with what is frivolous or ephemeral, and there is an assumption that as one grows older they are put aside for more serious pursuits, except very occasionally (as in the case with Art Spiegelman's *Maus*) when a forbiddingly grim subject is treated by a serious comic book artist. (Said, i)

Notwithstanding its ubiquitous nature graphic tales have found it difficult to be accepted as a serious form of writing among the readers. One could argue that this is due to an age-old binary between words and pictures in which the former is rated higher than the latter. But, that may not be entirely true as the readers always take time to warm up to anything new. One is reminded of the early days of novel writing when the pioneering novelists had to battle to have their art form accepted as legitimate. In Henry Fielding's *Tom Jones* (1749) one could read alongside the journey of the novel's hero to find his birthright a parallel journey taken by the nascent genre to legitimize itself. The graphic narrative is also on a similar journey and it is with the complexly rich and varied works of some exceptionally talented graphic artists like Will Eisner, Art Spiegelman, Joe Sacco, Guy Deslile, Alison Bechdel, Marjane Satrapi, etc. that the seriousness of the genre is getting registered among the readers.

My argument here must include two disclaimers. One, when I say graphic narrative to be a new genre I am not discounting a very old tradition of writing comics. Though many creators of graphic narrative would not accept any difference between comics and graphic narratives, one can still draw a line to categorize the more serious narratives as something different from the simpler comic strips we all loved during childhood. The term 'graphic novel' was coined in 1964 by Richard Kyle in the November issue of the newsletter *CAPA-alpha*. Originally the term was meant to denote a high quality of production and long length of narratives. In 1978, the term gained further currency when Will Eisner used it on the cover of his fictional work *A Contract with God and Other Tenement Stories*. Since then the term has been meant by the creators and readers to differentiate 'serious' artistic works from lighter works intended solely for entertainment. Like the comics, graphic novels use the same sequential art form but are differentiated by their complex themes and serious subject matters. Eddie Campbell elucidates the term 'graphic novel':

> The term graphic novel is currently used in at least four different and mutually exclusive ways. First it is used simply as a synonym for comic books.... Second it is used to classify a format—for example, a bound book of comics either in soft or hard cover—in contrast to the old fashioned stapled comic magazine. Third it means more specifically, a comic book narrative that is equivalent in form and dimensions to the prose novel. Finally others employ it to indicate a form that is more than a comic book in the scope of its ambition—indeed a new medium altogether. (13)

But even if one does not want to accede to the difference between comics and graphic narratives, one must revise the traditional way of considering comics as a lowbrow genre. Hillary Chute, in her essay titled "Comics as Literature? Reading Graphic Narrative", contends that to "explore today's comics we need to go beyond pre-established rubrics: we have to reexamine the categories of fiction, narrative, and historicity. Scholarship on comics—and specifically on what I will call graphic narrative—is gaining traction in the humanities" (452).

A part of Chute's contention is related to the second disclaimer. Many of the creators of graphic narratives, exceptional artists, would not bother about the academic acceptance of their art, about 'gaining traction in the humanities'. But academic acceptance and critical acclaim are necessary for a new genre to get established and the recent academic attention is doing the graphic narratives more good than harm. It is encouraging to note that over the last few years the universities have started offering courses on graphic literature and a heartening thing about this is that the academia is not including graphic art merely as making claims in the name of popular culture but to delve deep into the visual component of hermeneutics; to research on the affective power of images. It is also pertinent to put forward this disclaimer as the editor of the academic volume thinks it fit, and perhaps necessary, to include an essay on graphic narratives.

Turning the attention back towards Ali one notices how effectively the small speech balloon reminds Sacco, and through him us, that it is almost impossible for us to imagine what he feels. I am going back to that panel because it underscores a major issue dealt which has inspired many graphic novelists; the concept of home. Today's world is streaked with multiple acts of migration, forced or willed. Our lives are spent negotiating between the journey away from home and efforts to return. Sacco is remarkable in setting many of his narratives in the conflicted war zones. Palestine has long witnessed the pitfalls of sustained political conflicts resulting in hundreds and thousands becoming homeless. Similarly, troubled zones like the Gaza strip, Goražde have formed the crux of Sacco's narratives. He is remarkable as he neither romanticizes suffering nor tries to legitimize violence. Daniel Worden contends:

> A pioneer of comic journalism, Sacco has made it clear that comics have a representative force that can counter the amnesiac present tense of our media environment, and his work stands as a testament to cartooning's power to

> depict layers of experience, history, feeling, and action on a single page, in a single panel. (3)

The layers of experience and history are indeed Sacco's area of engagement and despite Ali's caveat that Sacco can't imagine what he feels comes very close in authentically feeling and representing the myriad experiences of war-torn individuals. Sacco combines two different types of writing; comics and journalism. This is an interesting combination as the former of these is traditionally taken to be light-hearted and frivolous while the latter is accepted to be realistic and truthful. Sacco had been trained in 'objective' reporting in the University of Oregon. In the Preface to his book *Journalism* (2012), Sacco notes how he had always felt differently about this objective reporting. In his well-known study *The Invention of Journalism Ethics*, Stephen A. Ward notes:

> The doctrine of journalism objectivity was invented in the 1920s—a North American invention of newspapers and journalism associations—after almost a century of anticipation in the popular press. Objectivity was never as popular in European journalism, where opinion continued to play a substantial role, even in news reporting. (214)

Objectivity in journalism requires neutrality on the part of the journalist. One may quote Ward again here: "The traditional language of journalistic objectivity is a normative language of self-denial, restraint, and exclusion. The reporter must, in an almost-Calvinist manner, keep a steady watch on his or her impulses to comment and interpret. Reporters provide an undistorted mirror on the world; they are passive recorders of facts" (20).

Sacco's attitude to journalism counters this neutrality which Ward recommends. He is rather in favour of an implied subjectivity which, according to him, articulates the role of social position and values. In *Journalism*, Sacco denies to accept the traditional mandate that journalists should approach a story with no preconceived idea. The presence of Sacco himself within the frames of his narratives automatically challenges the notion of objective journalism. This is an interesting choice. Isabel Macdonald observes:

> Sacco's bold move to draw himself into his journalism addresses one of the major weaknesses that have been observed in journalism's traditional theoretical framework. In light of growing awareness of how knowledge is influenced by the values and culture of those producing it, the notion that journalists can be neutral, objective observers is increasingly recognized as a myth. More specifically, Sacco's move to acknowledge his position as a foreign reporter is significant in light of the particular shortcomings "objective reporting" presents in the field of international reporting. (55)

Sacco discards this method of objective reporting and "embraces the implications of subjective reporting" (Sacco, *Journalism*, xiii). Explaining his decision to draw himself in the narratives Sacco claims that it gives himself "journalistic permission to show [his] interactions with those [he] meet[s]. Much can be learned from these personal exchanges, which most mainstream newspaper reporters, alas, excise from their articles" (xiii). This enquiry into the micro narratives of the people's lives, the people who are not merely objects of reporting for him, lends to Sacco's exploration a new historicist dimension which lays bare the hollow nooks of any macro narrative.

The subjects of Sacco's enquiry are lost in the intricate nets of politics and end up losing home and identity both at the metaphorical and literal levels. Home for the people is both a physical space to inhabit and a trope. Contemporary literature records the myriad acts of migration that define modern life. Graphic narratives too are alive to these significant aspects of the contemporary world. Over the years the artists have produced some telling works of graphic narrative art which have approached the question of home and identity from multifarious perspectives. Sacco, however, may not come automatically to the mind of a follower of graphic narratives when the issue of home is mentioned. Alison Bechdel's *Fun Home* (2006), on the other hand, instantly evokes the connection between the issue of home and graphic narratives. One may also apparently recall Art Spiegleman's *Maus: A Survivor's Tale* (1986); Marjane Satrapi's *Persepolis* (2008) or Gene Leun Yang's *American Born*

Chinese (2006). The Indian readers of graphic narratives can additionally recall *This Side, That Side: Restorying Partition* (2013), an anthology of twenty-eight short graphic narratives curated by Vishwajyoti Ghosh and Malik Sajad's *Munnu: A Boy from Kashmir* (2015).

Fun Home is a tragicomic memoir charting in a non-linear manner the growing up years of Alison and her siblings in Beech Creek. The narrative explores intimate and complex issues like gender roles; family's dysfunctional nature; emotional abuse and the role that literature can play in helping one make sense of one's life. All these are unfolded in the Victorian house of the Bechdels. Bechdel treats this house "not [as] an inert box" as the "Inhabited space transcends geometrical space" (Bachelard 47). Gaston Bachelard in *The Poetics of Space* (1958) and Amos Rapoport in *House Form and Culture* (1969) talk of space as a dwelling of human consciousness which combines the physical dimension of the house with the abstract concept of home.

Home is the most significant aspect of Spiegelman's seminal graphic novel *Maus* which records the experience of Spiegelman's parents during the World War II in Poland and his own struggle to come to terms with the identity of a second-generation Holocaust survivor. The novel is noted for its dense black and white panels, intermixing of different time frames within the same panel and allegorical representation of humans as animals. In evidencing the horrors of Holocaust *Maus* remains a burning testimony of human beings grappling with the question of identity in a world which have rendered them homeless. Satrapi's *Persepolis* tells the story of her childhood and growth in modern Iran in the time after the Shah and during the blooming power of Islamic fundamentalists. The narrative closely observes young Marjane's struggles to negotiate with the identity crisis arising out of her clash with the fundamentalist forces; her going away from her home and her return.

Like Satrapi's ethnic autobiography Luen Yang's *American Born Chinese* also concerns itself with the question of home and identity encountered by the members of the diasporic communities. The novel alternates among three spatio-temporally diverse narratives. The first of these is about the rise to power, downfall, and intellectual reawakening of the mythological Monkey King; the second is about the Chinese American Jin Wang's experiences of assimilating into the American school system and dealing with the traumas of adolescence; while the third concerns itself with the slapstick adventures of Danny, a white American teenager who represents Jin's fantasy self, and his visiting cousin Chin-Kee, whose exaggeratedly stereotypical traits repeatedly humiliate him. The novel explores a very relevant aspect of the diasporic existence—the conflict between the usually dissimilar cultures of the homeland and the host-land. Yang asserts that Jin must learn to accept his ethnic traditions and cultural roots and should never feel ashamed of his ethnic roots and avoid being scornful to his fellow Asians.

Ghost's *This Side, That Side* is innovatively designed with twenty-eight short graphic narratives address different aspects of partition and captures the trauma of this massive historical moment from diverse locations such as India, Pakistan and Bangladesh. In his review for kitaab.org Zafar Anjum observes that in the volume "[a] gamut of experiences of Partition are represented: life in refugee camps, the continuing difficulty of India-Pakistan cross-border travel, homelessness in both the physical and the psychological senses, the fundamental similarities between Indians, Pakistanis and Bangladeshis, despite political rhetoric" (kitaab.org). Though the tales at times appear to be without focus and clarity the stories (usually collaborations between writers and illustrators) underscore the nerve-wrecking and earth-shattering nature of the experience of being driven away from one's home. Sajad's *Munnu* is again concerned with the question of home and the loss of it. It tells the story of the Kashmiri people who are suffering from contradictory national and political pulls. Like Maus *Munnu* also portrays humans as animals—an endangered species of a deer. Taking the side of the Kashmiris and looking at the depleted situation of this naturally beautiful province through the eyes of the young boy Munnu Sajad depicts conflict-torn individuals reeling under the overbearing sense of the loss of home.

Sacco's *Palestine* is a gripping work of art constituted of interviews conducted and observations made by the author during his stay in the winter of 1991-92 in the Palestinian territories occupied by Israel. The narrative takes the readers from the first Palestinian Intifada in 1987 against Israeli military occupation to the time when it subsided in 1992. Palestine opens with an image of Sacco with his back to us looking through the gap between walls to the city landscape marked by buildings rising low. This is an important insight into Sacco's approach to story-telling; he is an observer who is also a participant. The novel further finds Sacco with two hotel receptionists. While one of them is in love the other talks about politics. This again is pertinent to the life Sacco draws, a life in which the personal and the political overlap. Sacco's mode of representation is marked not only by his engagement with his subjects but also with that of the readers of his work. Reviewing *Palestine* for *The Arab Studies Journal* Bhakti Shringarpure contends:

> The book itself commands involvement as the reader gets the full blast of drawings and writing, ranging from conventional rows of box frames to the frame-less slanting images, to large panoramas, to long horizontal strips. It keeps the reader involved and uncomfortable since it becomes imperative to twist and turn the book at various angles during the reading process. The whole work has an underlying seething quality, with images that feel inherently volatile and about to leap into violent movement. It conveys the instability and the unpredictably of life in Palestine. (215)

Palestine is remarkable for its portrayal of lived reality and Sacco lives up to the demands of such portrayal by being sensitive and truthful to his role of a mediator. But he is not a typical mediator and he keeps questioning the nature of journalism through self-mockery. This self-mocking enables him to have a comprehensive understanding of the reality he is representing. He does not euphemize or hide the conflicts. The reader experiences the disparities that exist between the Israelis and the Palestinians in every sphere of the society wherein even the law treats them differently. Towards the end of *Palestine* Sacco meets two Israeli women who talk of their dislike of violence. These sequences are followed up with panels comprising of Palestinians encountering violence everywhere. The Israelis can exercise choices whereas for the Palestinians violence is not a matter of choice but thrust upon them. Choice is not an option for the Palestinians who feel homeless in their homeland. Said's observation on Sacco's representational skill may be quoted here:

> There's no obvious spin, no easily discernible line of doctrine in Joe Sacco's often ironic encounters with the Palestinians under occupation, no attempt to smooth out what is for the most part a meager, anxious existence of uncertainty, collective unhappiness, and deprivation, and, especially in the Gaza comics, a life of aimless wandering within the place's inhospitable confines, wandering and mostly waiting, waiting, waiting. (iii)

Sacco does not mince his words and *Palestine* remains in the hands of its engaged author a call for action; a call to the reader to step up to the massive injustice that is going around.

However, such involvement may be questioned by traditional journalism which calls for disengaged mediation. Sacco, being influenced by alternative journalistic styles of George Orwell, Michael Herr and Hunter S. Thompson (Marshall, 22-23), is willing to challenge the traditional modes of reportage. In an interview given to Mother Jones magazine Sacco talks about the necessity of journalism to respond to the demands created by what he calls the 'visual world':

> It's a visual world and people respond to visuals. With comics you can put interesting and solid information in a format that's pretty palatable. For me, one advantage of comic journalism is that I can depict the past, which is hard to do if you're a photographer or filmmaker. History can make you realize that the present is just one layer of a story. What seems to be the immediate and vital story now will one day be another layer in this geology of bummers. (Cited by Worden, 7)

This historical sense lends to Sacco's journalism a wider arc not addressed by the demands of temporality on mainstream journalism. Sacco's art lies in making the reader empathize with his subjects. But it would be a mistake to suppose that Sacco is all about feeling for his narratives are well researched and help the readers not only to garner a lot of information about the places he paints but also acquire knowledge about it.

I have noted earlier that Sacco combines the personal with the political. I may here add that Sacco guides the reader through the personal to the historical, to a comprehensive understanding of the precarious plights of his subjects in relation to the bigger picture. This move from the personal to the historical can be traced to the influence of Michael Herr and his New Journalism on Sacco. In his edited volume *New Journalism* (1973; co-edited with E.W. Johnson) Tom Wolfe notes how the New Journalists engaged with the structural and the personal as they were

> moving beyond the conventional limits of journalism, but not merely in terms of technique. The kind of reporting they were doing struck them as far more ambitious, too. It was more intense, more detailed, and certainly more time-consuming than anything that newspaper or magazine reporters, including investigative reporters, were accustomed to. They developed the habit of staying with the people they were writing about for days at a time, weeks in some cases. They had to gather all the material the conventional journalist was after—and then keep going. It seemed all-important to *be there* when dramatic scenes took place, to get the dialogue, the gestures, the facial expressions, the details of the environment. The idea was to give the full objective description, plus something that readers had always had to go to novels and short stories for: namely, the subjective or emotional life of the characters. (20-21)

Joe Sacco is remarkable in fusing such alternative modes of journalism with his graphic art and demands by his own right to be taken seriously. *Safe Area Goražde* is demands special attention. Unlike *Palestine*, which was serialized from 1993 to 1995, it was published as a single long graphic narrative in 2000. It was still divided in chapters and comprised of interviews but one could notice that in *Safe Area Goražde* Sacco has moved away from his autobiographical approach to concentrate chiefly on representing how the complex history of the area has led to the contemporary political crisis.

Safe Area Goražde: The War in Eastern Bosnia 1992-1995 is set against the backdrop of Goražde, a United Nations designated "safe area". Located on the banks of Drina river (which forms a large portion of the border between Bosnia and Herzegovina and Serbia), this Muslim-dominated settlement is surrounded by Serb-controlled regions and had been constantly under attack since the beginning of the war since 1992 resulting in the segregation of the town with its 57,000 residents from the rest of the world. The book is based on Sacco's multiple trips to Goražde between late 1995 and early 1996 and is divided in twelve chapters of varied length. Sacco focuses on the lives of the local inhabitants and refugees to explore their lived experience; their memories of war; the lasting impact of multiple military attacks and the international attention, or the lack of it, to the situation.

In the opening chapter titled "Go Away" Sacco uses two splash pages, one beginning the chapter the other ending. In the opening splash (which is also used as the cover page for the book) shows a convoy of tankers and trucks moving towards Goražde, a town of charred houses clearly bearing the marks of bullets and bombs. The hills in the distance offer no relief and are marked with the sign "No-man's-land". In the foreground the narrative reads; "In the fall of 1995, the future of Goražde and its 57,000 inhabitants was by no means clear..." (1). This convoy may enkindle the hope of international attention and care. But Sacco undercuts any such hope as the closing splash page of the chapter strikingly lays bare the opposite. It shows a crowd of people, ranging from young to old, looking with expectation across a road scarred with mine explosion. Guarding them there are a handful of soldiers carrying guns. The trees are absolutely bare again highlighting that nature does not play any nourishing role here. On the foreground Sacco tellingly places a young boy with crutches. There is only one small narrative card used at the foreground; "'I wish Goražde would go away,' I heard one American correspondent say..." (4). The splash page arrests the readers with its minimum use of words to evoke the helpless scenario the locals are caught in and the lack of empathy showed by media which is there to mediate between them and the world outside. One may quote the words of Hillary Chute here: "In his *Safe Area Goražde,* Sacco spatializes the elliptical prose style of avant-garde writers such as Louis-Ferdinand Céline, fragmenting boxes of text and floating them over his images. Spatializing the verbal narrative to dramatize or disrupt the visual narrative threads ellipses into the grammar of a medium already characterized by the elliptical structure of the frame-gutter-frame sequence" (460).

In the same essay Chute further comments: "We may note such an example in one of Sacco's most disturbing pages in *Safe Area Goražde*, which represents the testimony of Sacco's Bosnian friend and translator Edin and depicts the dead bodies of Edin's friends, four men who died in the first day of the first Serb attack on Goražde in May 1992" (460). The readers encounter in the panels a row of dead bodies with Edin identifying his friends; "Izet's son Rofa, was with me in school for 12 years. There was dirt in his stomach. Probably they'd cut open his stomach. Senad was with me four years in the same class. Senad's fingers had been cut from one hand, the other was shut tight. All of them were without penises" (93). Sacco uses black gutters for the survivors' tales demarcating them from the usual white gutters to denote the darkness which engulfs the lives of these survivors. Sacco juxtaposes the inanimate with the living to provide a comprehensive picture of the devastations witnessed by Goražde. In the chapter titled "15 Minutes" one finds a half-page long panel with a bombed out school-building. The narrative reads, "This secondary school, one of three in Goražde, had been gutted" (97). One chapter later we encounter Rasim, a refugee from Visegrad and an eyewitness to massacres in 1992. In the chapter "Around Goražde Part I" we find Rasim, in a number of panels, facing directly the readers while recounting the bitter experiences. In the following chapter titled "Around Goražde Part II" Sacco uses the same technique to recount the harrowing experiences of Munira, another refugee from the village of Kapov Han. She was taken to "the special department for pregnant women at Foca" (117) where she found women, many of them pregnant or have just delivered babies, taken by Chetnik soldiers to be raped. Facing the readers directly in more than one panel Munira's tale lays bare the horrors of sexual assault. Surrounded in black gutters these panels make one face the unrelieved horror faced by these people.

Along with these gripping tales of the survivors Sacco goes on providing the readers with information about the war, the political conflicts. In chapters of Edin's memoir and that of Bahra we get to know how the "Axis powers...installed Croatian fascists, the Utasha" which led to the formation of "two competing resistance groups, the Chetniks and the Partisans.... The Chetniks waged a ruthless war against Bosnia's Croat and Muslim citizenry" (21). We get to know how "[w]ar broke out in north-eastern Bosnia in the towns of Bijeljina and Zovnik in early April 1992" (41). We are told how ethnic cleansing of non-Serb inhabitants began. The Serb bombardment began with the Bosnian Government unprepared to fight the war. The trauma of war never leaves us and though at times one salutes the spirit of the people of Goražde like Riki we are never allowed to forget the horrors of war.

The war in Bosnia happened with the media covering almost every bit of it. Susan Sontag observes, "Unlike the genocide of the Armenians during World War I and of the Jews and the Gypsies in the late 1930s and early 1940s, the genocide of the Bosniak people has taken place in the glare of worldwide press and TV coverage" (Cited by Dong 46). Sacco concentrates on how the people are misrepresented by the media which is mostly interested in itself. In a striking panel Sacco paints how journalists ruthlessly cover the 'news' by drawing them talking to the camera and holding microphones before a kid while in the background the people of Goražde stand as onlookers. Sacco's narrative reads: "Goražde...had just wrested the spotlight from that media darling Sarajevo!...which was getting CNNed! NPRed! BBCed!... But its proverbial 15 minutes were ticking away" (6). In another sequence Sacco meets the students in Edin's class. When they were requested to ask him questions one of them asked, "Why did you come to Goražde?" (13). Following this there is a two-page spread showing a usual day in Goražde unfolding against a town with marks of devastation. Herein Sacco answers in fragmented narrative, "Why?/ Because you are still here/ not raped and scattered/ not entangled in the limbs of thousands of others at the bottom of a pit/ Because Goražde had lived, and—/ How?" (14-15).

Indeed, it is significant to know how Goražde had lived through the trauma of war and conflict. From experiencing the "greatest mass killing in Europe in 50 years" which found "more than 7000 Muslim men" shot by "the Serbs in the break-out to Tuzla" (203) to witnessing the Balkan leaders signing a peace settlement Goražde has seen it all. But such peace comes at a heavy price as we find in the Epilogue many of Goražde relocating to Sarajevo. But even that does not promise a settled future. The loss of home can never be completely compensated with and leaves a permanent scar for the war-affected people.

In Goražde time almost stands still making apparent its difference from the world outside. The constant presence of the media people and their airing the news from the place produce a semblance of temporal connectivity with the world but time does not move in Goražde. This arrested quality of time is best captured by Sacco's description of Edin who, after completed all the courses, didn't have the opportunity to defend his thesis (which requires 15 minutes) to be awarded his degree in mechanical engineering. Sacco writes; Edin had "been 15 minutes from his degree for the past three and a half years" (98). Sacco's representation of the lives of the people of Goražde captures the essence of being cut off from the external world. Compared with earlier times the majority of the recent causalities of war are civilians. Thinking in this light Sacco's emphasis on recording the narratives of civilians of this war-conflicted zone assumes pertinent dimension. Alla Gadassik and Sarah Henstra argue that "Sacco's driving question isn't just how to tell the silenced stories but how to approach the subject most ethically, given the conflicting interests.... Rather than asking readers to accept the truth of his account, he constructs a narrative that encourages us actively to interpret and reflect on what we're reading" (246). These silent stories need a voice to be articulated and Sacco, with his empathy and participatory quality, provides that.

In the section marked "Prologue" a man comes to Sacco with a manuscript on the situation in Goražde and claims to know the real truth about Goražde. But Sacco is wise enough to know that there cannot be any one real truth about anything. *Safe Area Goražde* invites the reader to journey with Sacco and the people 'safe in the area' to experience his own truth and form his own understanding. In portraying this multifarious nature of truth Sacco is helped by the form of his art which fuses journalism and comics to lend authenticity to the narrative and helps drive home the truth(s). Such a fusion of two apparently disparate modes of articulation does neither take the seriousness away from the subjects represented nor dilutes the authenticity. We may conclude with Rocco Versaci's words from his study *This Book Contains Graphic Language*:

> Comics journalists have taken full advantage of the graphic language of the medium to reanimate the most salient feature of New Journalism: the foregrounding of the individual perspective as an organizing consciousness. In addition, comics journalists achieve layers of meaning inaccessible to prose journalism alone because of comics' graphic language that blends words and images. What is more, like the New Journalists, comics journalists embrace a pointed anti-"official" and anticorporate attitude. However, unlike the absorption of New Journalism into the mainstream and the resulting dilution of its radical message, comics journalism retains, paradoxically, a powerful marginal status that will make it difficult for these works to ever be fully "co-opted". (111)

Works Cited

Anjum, Zafar. Kitaab Review: *This Side, That Side: Restorying Partition*. kitaab.org. Web.

Bachelard, Gaston. *The Poetics of Space*. 1958. Trans. Maria Jolas. Boston: Beacon Press, 1969. Print.

Campbell, Eddie. "What is a Graphic Novel?". *World Literature Today*, Vol. 81, No. 2, Graphic Literature (Mar.-Apr. 2007). 13-15. Print.

Chute, Hillary. "Comics as Literature? Reading Graphic Narrative". *PMLA*, Vol. 123, No. 2 (Mar. 2008). 452-65. Print.

Dong, Lan. "Inside and Outside the Frame: Joe Sacco's *Safe Area Goražde*". *The Comics of Joe Sacco: Journalism in a Visual World*. Ed. Daniel Worden. Jackson: UP of Mississippi, 2015. 39-53. Print.

Gadassik, Alla and Sarah Henstra. "Comics (as) Journalism: Teaching Joe Sacco's *Palestine* to Media Students," *Teaching Comics and Graphic Narratives: Essays on Theory, Strategy and Practice*. Ed. Lan Dong. Jefferson, NC: McFarland, 2012. 243-59. Print.

Macdonald, Isabel. "Drawing on the Facts: Comics Journalism and the Critique of Objectivity". *The Comics of Joe Sacco: Journalism in a Visual World*. Ed. Daniel Worden. Jackson: UP of Mississippi, 2015. 54-66. Print.

Marshall, Monica. *Joe Sacco*. New York: Rosen, 2005. Print.

Sacco, Joe. *Notes From a Defeatist*. Seattle: Fantagraphic Book, 2003. Print.

———. *Palestine*. Seattle: Fantagraphic Book, 2003. Print.

———. *Safe Area Goražde: The War in Eastern Bosnia 1992-1995*. 2000. London: Jonathan Cape, 2007. Print.

———. "A Manifesto, Anyone?" *Journalism*. New York: Metropolitan, 2012. xi-xiv. Print.

Said, Edward. "Introduction". *Palestine*. Seattle: Fantagraphic Book, 2003. i-v. Print.

Shringarpure, Bhakti. Review Essay. *The Arab Studies Journal*. Vol. 11/12, No. 2/1 (Fall 2003/Spring 2004). 212-17. Print.

Versaci, Rocco. *This Book Contains Graphic Language: Comics as Literature*. London: Bloomsbury, 2007. Print.

Ward, Stephen J.A. *The Invention of Journalism Ethics: The Path to Objectivity and Beyond*. Kingston, Canada: McGill-Queen's University Press, 2004. Print.

Wolfe, Tom. "The New Journalism". *The New Journalism*. Eds. Tom Wolfe and E.W. Johnson. New York: Harper and Row, 1973. 20-21. Print.

Worden, Daniel. Ed. *The Comics of Joe Sacco: Journalism in a Visual World*. Jackson: UP of Mississippi, 2015. Print.

15

Anxiety of Acceptance: Recent Popular Representations of Gothic on Screen

Nivedita Bachhar

The term 'Gothic' has its roots from the barbaric races of the Goths invading the Roman Civilization and pushing westwards in Europe. Pillage and destruction which accompanied the invasions, is the source of association with death. The Gothic tribes also brought with them a particular form of architecture of those races that was prominently distinguishable and different from that of the medieval architecture. This new form was distinguished in designs of engineering which allowed structures of high ceilings and marked by pointed turrets which often create a play of light and shade creating somber ambience of mystery. Gothic is also connected to the iconoclastic tendencies during Reformation and Counter-Reformation which referred to the destruction of icons in the churches; motion against religion especially, at that particular era would require a certain amount of spirit which in our time can be equated with rebelliousness.

Later, during the quest for newer forms in literature, all the above took a new shape in the Romantic imagination as they delved into the past in search for something sensational to cater to the emerging bigger size of readers. With Horace Walpole's *The Castle of Otranto: A Gothic Story,* set in Walpole's own Gothic Strawberry Hill, the term merges with a particular genre of Romantic Novel featuring sliding panels, moving doors, dark secret corridors, unnatural or supernatural beings, love-triangles, cruel and vicious villains, often equally vicious female protagonists and the cumulative effects intends to, as a number of writers had said, "Chill the spine and curdle the blood".

In spite of the emergence of various genres, the interest in the Gothic in the 20th century and the 21st century remains unaffected. In fact, many men of letters in the period in between, including Edmund Burke or Walter Scott have confessed to spending hours reading the Gothic. Rather, in the course of its evolution, the Gothic has evolved as a genre of greater seriousness still manifesting the essentially same features; it has become more complex, the illustration of which is tangible in the pop culture extending to music and fashion. Various forms of sexuality, the rights of the subalterns and complex problems of a social nature, are quite discernible under the surface, as are the various psychological complexities. They are essentially human problems, but are amplified to fantastic dimensions. Perhaps, these dynamic factors account for the unwavering popularity of even the television shows and films of questionable qualities.

One of the chief psychological issues, which are recurrent in most of the Gothic on screen is the anxiety of loneliness. This is, needless to say, a common situation, but severely amplified and problematized by the ideas of eternity and immortality. The fear of being socio-politically ostracized plays a major role in every human life; the complexities surrounding the evolution of relations often result in separation and formation of new relations—both in the personal and collective levels. This is an inevitable process. But what happens in case of special individuals who are social misfits and hence not easily able to foster new relationships? What happens if the individual has to live eternally in perpetual loneliness by loss of a companion or simply from not being able to relate and connect? This is where the modern vampire myths, in fact, most contemporary supernatural myths, become relevant. The eternity metaphor becomes an amplifier of the problems faced by the individual. The uniqueness of the person as an individual pushed to the periphery of acceptability becomes well captured in the tenets of the vampire construct. Thereby, the qualities one associate with vampires become, more than ever, the expression of the problems that the 'unique' faces these days.

Another feature distinguishing the Gothic of the Victorian period from Bram Stoker's *Dracula* from the Gothic of the late

20th century is the recurrent plot in vampire stories where the vampires try to overcome their monstrosity finding alternative sources of nutritional sustenance projecting themselves as milder beings sometimes even capable of altruism. Along with this, these individuals, incapable of reproduction, very often flock together, fostering familial relationships creating their 'home'. Not only that, often, they even form alternative society inclusive of the social constructs of their own set of rules and laws with the primary agenda of survival and peaceful cohabitation with the humans where again deviation can bring a penalty extending to even death sentence. This can be translated as a quest for alternative identity and also an attempt of construction of an alternative 'home' where the 'unacceptable' create or endeavor to create a separate space for themselves.

In this context, references can be made to a few popular Gothic on screen representations taken from the shows which span over the last two decades. The cinematic adaptations often do not translate on screen as per the locus of the plot in the books; but such deviation is inevitable in any adaptation, especially, from one medium into another. The cinematic adaptations may be more deserving as they gained interesting popularity which goes beyond the book-reading audience. Their aesthetic merit as cinema and TV serial is a matter of discussion beyond the scope of this paper. Even though these adaptations may not always deserve the so-called serious academic consideration, still, they contain elements which are socially relevant. Only the most relevant details from the plots are examined here.

In *An Interview with the Vampire: Vampire Chronicles*, the anxiety of relations and the fear of loneliness is the most apparent. It is one of the central themes. Louis, an indigo-planter had been turned into a vampire by Lestat who desires Louis to be his companion. Together, they create havoc. Louis is appalled by his own life of murder and loneliness which he has to bear into eternity. Lestat creates a child-monster Claudia to give Louis a daughter.

Claudia in course of time realizes that although psychologically she has matured into a woman, physically she is still a child which depresses and throws her into a fit of anger.

She also becomes appalled by the realization of the monstrosity of killing humans randomly which Lestat had taught her as a child and having no sense of right and wrong because of her immaturity, she had taken to it quickly. As a means of escape and revenge, she tried to poison Lestat. Later, Louis depressed by their own life, tries to part ways and Claudia cries out that he is the father, brother, lover, in short, the only companion in her lonely life. They travel to Europe and meet Armand and his coven in Paris where they experience similar mindless murders; they try leaving in disgust. In their bid of simulating a complete family, they bring in a new member, a mother. But, even for the subversive, the endeavor of subversion is unacceptable. Lestat returns and incites the Parisian vampire coven who readily acts against Louis and his new family imprisoning him in a coffin for life (Armand rescues him later) and exposing Claudia and her new mother to sunlight to burn into ashes. This is of course the issue of forceful inclusion which happens in case of marginalized or dislocated communities. The resentment of the 'relocated' is a significant pointer towards the unacceptability of the individuals or the isolated community they represent.

The scene of Claudia's death not only rouses pathos of the situation but overwhelming pain and fear of loneliness to be borne into eternity engulfs Louis and it seems to affect the audience as well. The much detested, unscrupulous Lestat returns and reflecting reality, the lonely does not have the choice of companions; he has to accept the rare few around. It seems, Louis also accepts Lestat back. In the interview, Louis tries to convey the pain. But when the interviewer admires the idea of power, eternity and knowledge and wishes to be turned into a vampire, Louis is enraged because the interviewer had failed to realize the pain and Louis has failed to communicate.

In *Twilight*, a similar motif of adoption of family and the quest for home is quite prominent. The Cullens constantly grow by virtue of adoptions creating all kinds of familial relations building their home.

The similar anxiety is covertly evident in *True Blood* which is rather more complex than any of the previous adaptations by the virtue or sin of political and social innuendos it posits. All the major characters are one or other kind of mythical beings. Of this variety of beings, only the vampires are the known kind to the humans. Even though they are part of the tax-paying population, they, like the African-Americans before the 1960s, do not posses either political and legal rights, nor protection. Even though they try to cohabit by surviving on the alternative to human blood, the synthetic *True Blood*, suspicions based on cultural and religious beliefs still prevail. In the series, all the misfits eventually flock together supporting each other. They represent the homeless who has no home anywhere. They, like in *An Interview with the Vampire*, simulate relations by adopting or creating 'progenies' and teaching, nurturing and protecting them. The 'creator', the human equivalent of 'father' is responsible for his progenies and is also connected telepathically to his progenies sensing their mental and physical situations even from far off.

It might be interesting to note in this context that even though these 'other' kind of individuals are tormented by loneliness, they do not attempt by volition to be accepted by the mainstream. This maintained distance between them and the rest creates a mystery and the glamorous aura—in *An Interview with the Vampire*, the reporter wishes to be turned into one; in *True Blood*, there are humans who voluntarily turn into vampires, in *Twilight* the heroine also sought to be one. Again, in each of these, even the loners gravitate as they struggle to find a home.

While this could be read as the subaltern finding a voice, this might also be read as an attempt of companionship of individuals who exist outside the realms of acceptance. It is a contradictory situation where the deviant but compromising attitude forward norms; while, on the other hand, digressive behavior delights in subversion of the norms. The norm itself does not compromise because the vampires still remain on the periphery of acceptability sometimes by volition and sometimes by circumstance.

Most works in the genre point to this anxiety which has been major, perhaps, even before the dawn of civilization when people lived in small groups and blending in was important for survival. The anxiety of acceptance and loneliness has become a rather psychological malady which engulfs the modern world. Fairy tales with the princes and damsels-in-distress no longer relate to the social texture. But the Gothic, with its dynamism adapts to the time. The constant struggle of the 'others' and the lonely individuals against the world of constant adversity, provides the solace and still somehow bears the hope of the 'happily ever after'. Therefore, popular culture now banks heavily on the Gothic to represent the voice of the other, the marginalized and the unaccepted.

Works Cited

Interview with the Vampire: Vampire Chronicles. Writ. Anne Rice. Dir. Neil Jordan. Perf. Brad Pitt, and Tom Cruise. Geffen Pictures. Worldwide, Nov. 1994. Film.

Twilight. Writ. Stephenie Meyer. Dir. Catherine Hardwicke. Perf. Kristen Stewart, and Robert Pattinson. Temple Hill Entertainment. USA, 21 Nov. 2008. Film.

True Blood: The Complete First Season. Dir. Alan Ball. HBO. USA, 7 Sept.-23 Nov. 2008. Television.

True Blood: The Complete Second Season. Dir. Daniel Minahan. HBO. USA, 14 Jun.-13 Sept. 2009. Television.

True Blood: The Complete Third Season. Dir. Daniel Minahan. HBO. USA, June 2010-12 Sept. 2010. Television.

True Blood: The Complete Fourth Season. Dir. Michael Lehmann. HBO. USA, 26 Jun. 2011-11 Sept. 2012. Television.

True Blood: The Complete Fifth Season. Dir. Daniel Minahan. HBO. USA, 10 Jun.-26 Aug. 2012. Television.

True Blood: The Complete Sixth Season. Dir. Stephen Moyer. HBO. USA, 16 Jun.-11 Aug. 2013. Television.

True Blood: The Complete Seventh Season. Dir. Stephen Moyer. HBO. USA, 22 Jun.-24 Aug. 2014. Television.

Brooks, Chris. *The Gothic Revival*. London: Phaidon, 1999. Print.

Cuddon, J.A. *Dictionary of Literary Terms and Literary Theory*.

Davenport-Hines, Richard. *Gothic: 400 Years of Excess, Horror, Evil and Ruin*. London: Fourth Estate, 1998. Print.

Ellis, Markman. *The History of Gothic Fiction*. Edinburgh: Edinburgh University Press, 2000. Print.

Gelder, Ken. *Reading the Vampire*. London: Routledge, 1994. Print.

Groom, Nick. *The Gothic: A Very Short Introduction*. United Kingdom: Oxford University Press, 2012. Print.

Heather, Peter. *The Goths*. Oxford: Blackwell, 1996. Print.

Kilgour, Maggie. *The Rise of the Gothic Novel*. Abingdon: Routledge, 1995. Print.

King, Stephen. *Danse Macabre*. London: Hodder, 1981. Print.

Punter, David, ed. *A Companion to Gothic Fiction*. Cambridge: Cambridge University Press, 2002. Print.

Sage, Victor, ed. *The Gothick Novel: A Selection of Essays*. Houndmills: The Macmillan Press Ltd., 1990. Print.

16

Outward Journey Inward: Blurred Boundaries in Italo Calvino's *If on a Winter's Night a Traveller*

Rishiraj Pal

A novel is a corporeal, palpable entity consisting of pages that house the narrative. However, the textual homeliness can only be conceived through a phenomenological exchange—the act of reading vis-à-vis a pedagogic obstacle designed by expectation and training. It is due to the manufactured desires and the semantic impulses that the act of reading involves the difference in pleasure gained by a faithful and that by a licentious reading. Deeming the novel as fugal, rather than teleological, my contention here shares the anxiety of the homely comfort that a realist narrative offers; it paradoxically engages in a teleological sojourn for the novel that the 'you' has begun to 'read', crossing many borders and journeying forth.

Genetic inquiries problematize the very 'home' of a literary work; when studied genetically even the most canonical of the works start to move, to migrate, leaving behind its imprints while acquiring newer meanings. Oscillating between the two poles inherent in genetic studies—the process by which the work came into being and the product that resulted—the work must then be understood as a part of a system comprising the experiential, the affective, and the allusive. There is usually no such thing as a consensus as to how the genetic methodologies are to be employed in a particular work. Procedural yet intuitive, the exercise brings us to a critical juncture: is the text always in motion travelling from one conceived experiential domain to a stranger one or it is merely an extension of the boundaries of our exegetic expectation? To understand this problematic in an actual literary work rather than in the 'avant-texte' consisting of all the documents facilitating the conception of a work, this essay aims to offer an insight into textual migration vis-à-vis Italo Calvino's *If on a Winter's Night a Traveller* (1979).

The playful narrative-carnival that the work eventually becomes subsumes the very possibility of an orderly home. Sudden leaps and jagged edges of the narrative frustrate our expectations. Frustrations function within a fetishized realm of pattern, of predictable denials. A strict pattern is born amidst the mob of possibilities. The newer trails make the search all the more chaotic and challenging. In this abundance of genetic information and possible directions that the journey can take, Reader-traveller is made to follow a particular line of investigation. Calvino understands the primacy of an order that marks even the most chaotic of processes:

> My procedure is different because I try to deepen the contrast between sentences that are apparently linear, classical, and a reality that is undeniably complex. In the end, I believe that all writers share this fundamental urge even when they represent the most chaotic of realities. Just as the fact of *writing* implies an order. (Lucente 253)

The difference is between the regular repetition of patterns and the rich, coherent variation of an artist's creation. Aperiodic disappearances and methodic absences in the range of narratives, the micro-texts, as it were, that the novel abounds in, are punctuated by periodic conjectures; a parallel narrative, which now might be considered as the macro-text, of the journey in search of the ur-text acknowledges the formation of what one would understand as an 'avant-texte'—all the documents that come before a work when it is considered as a text and when those documents and the text are considered as part of a system. According to Jean Bellemin-Noel, "We must never forget this paradox: what was written *before* and had, at first, no after, we meet only after, and this tempts us to supply a before in the sense of a priority, cause, or origin" (Bellemin-Noel 31).

A home in this context of textual conception is that point of origin, the premise, in reference to which the movements and oscillations are measured. Allowing a text to assume anthropomorphic proportions, Calvino runs the risk of opening up a trail for the elusive origin(al). It migrates into various unknown, obscure terrains; it percolates though the porous national boundaries and takes refuge into the places most hostile for a reader to trace it down. As Professor Uzzi-Tuzii elaborates in his lecture:

> Reading...is always this: there is a thing that is there, a thing made of writing, a solid, material object, which cannot be changed, and through this thing we measure ourselves against something else that is not present, something else that belongs to the immaterial, invisible world, because it can only be thought, imagined, or because it was once and is no longer, past, lost, unattainable, in the land of the dead.... (Calvino 72)

Home, more often than not, suggests a familiar 'inside' which should be pitted against, if not a completely unfamiliar, but definitely an obtrusive, 'outside'. They are in an overdetermined relationship rather than in a dialectical one. To understand this construction of an 'outside' within the home, the modalities of composition would act as a necessary premise. However directional and logical a path it must take, it allows confusion and uncertainties to take over. It is a labyrinthine journey which foregrounds the importance of an origin and a destination. Calvino, in this novel, which uses metacommentary with such flamboyance that self-reflexivity becomes obvious, suggests a circular journey as far as the traveller-reader is concerned; he comes back to the familiar library that his city owns, only to find out all the titles, that he has stumbled upon during his search for the discontinued narratives, to be available right there. The *outside* has always been in the home. The home was never lost; it has been diffused in the outside through the author's ludic impetus:

> Reader, it is time for your tempest-tossed vessel to come to port. What harbor can receive you more securely than a great library? Certainly there is one in the city from which you set out and to which you have returned after circling the world from book to book. (Calvino 253)

The clues, that lead all the readers to the same library at the end, have facilitated a detour, and in doing so has heightened, what it must, the suspense. What one might wonder at this satisfying moment of resolution is the problematic relationship between the home and the point of origin, between the authentic and the dubious. Home, in his case, therefore ceases to be a space, or for that matter a place, from which one is exiled or alienated. An outside is invented to validate the homely, familiar narrative. The search for the story has always been a centripetal search for the Reader's self that has been caught and captivated in the story he has begun to read. It is as if he is alienated from himself. This is not only a search for the story but also for the Self that suffers a rupture when it fails to identify with the story he wishes to continue reading. Julia Kristeva in *Strangers to Ourselves* discusses this phenomenon at length: "...foreignness, an uncanny one, creeps into the tranquillity of reason itself.... Henceforth, we know that we are foreigners to ourselves, and it is with the help of that sole support that we can attempt to live with others" (Kristeva 170).

Is the Reader not only the reader but a piece of 'you' in the novelistic space? Is the reader *of* the novel travelling or 'you', the Reader, *in* the novel? Does he leave the comfort of his home to find the narrative, the original story, or has the narrative migrated into other forms of writings, crossing the boundaries of genres? To make matters complicated, as a metafictional narrative is likely to do, Calvino designs the narrative as a romance, where the drive to find the homely can be understood as a drive to get back to that point of primordial existence, to the beginning, to unite with the unconscious projections that the desire to attain the estranged storyline has produced. It is precisely why the novel ends with the line, "Just a moment, I've almost completed reading *If on a Winter's Night a Traveller* by Italo Calvino" (Calvino 300). The search has ended in an uncanny manner:

> Uncanny is something which is secretly familiar, which has undergone repression and then returned from it.... Uncanny is in reality nothing new or alien but which is familiar and old-established in the mind and which has

> become alienated from it only through the process of repression. (Freud 217)

The network of lines has intersected facilitating the rehabilitation of the once-dislocated being, which is "the form of a returning to place, a re-finding of oneself, a reorientation (even, perhaps, a repositioning)—as Heidegger himself refers to it, a form of homecoming, although a coming-home to that from which we never really departed" (Malpas 111). It is in this 'event' of homecoming that the narrative in Calvino indulges in another deception: we, the readers, know at the end of the novel how the story is traced down but not the story itself; paradoxically the story of the novel is about the tracing down the original story; no more, no less. All the other documents that have been rummaged only to arrive with more clues, albeit all the more deceitful, shape up the genetic schema. Being at home with the story is infused with the threats and confusions that being in the world in search of the story would entail. There are many instances when the content, along with all its uncertainties, complements the form with such wit and finesse that only Calvino's self-reflexivity can afford: "The novel begins in a railway station, a locomotive huffs, steam from a piston covers the opening of the chapter, a cloud of smoke hides part of the first paragraph" (Calvino 10).

Toying with this gulf between what *happens* in the story and what the story *is*, Calvino almost "asserts the resistance of fact to fiction, human freedom and unpredictability against plot" (Kermode 113). Chapter Two furthers the actual novel by offering a break; what the gullible Reader naively understood to be a first few pages of the titular story, is actually only one of those unfinished microtexts that the novel is made up of. Being vulnerable to the inertia of reading, the Reader now wants to go back to the embryonic comfort, to get nourished by the homely, familiar patterns of storytelling. It is a journey both away from the lost home—the familiar mode narrative and the actual story that has lost itself midway in the printing-binding mishap—and towards a home that preserves the actual story. There is a constant tension between the actual and the accidental; the skilled concoction of narratives is passed off as chances and coincidences of a quest.

One is aware of the fact that *If on a Winter's Night a Traveller* is not only a self-conscious narrative; it is a novel about a quest for a story, a particular book. The Reader has travelled to very many places and crossed many boundaries to arrive at a destination. Was he travelling away from his perceived home only to find his authentic/ideal home? The traveller of the first story seems to have passed the baton to the Reader who now travels for the original story, the one he started reading; it is now the story of the Reader(s): "Oh, the traveler only appeared in the first few pages and then was never mentioned again—he had fulfilled his function, the novel wasn't his story..." (Calvino 259).

Apparently there seems to be two kinds of journey: firstly, the reader(s) travel to myriad places to track down the story that they have started to read. And, secondly, the journey that the story undertakes from "If on a Winter's Night a Traveller" to 'What story down there awaits its end?' However, there is another journey that follows the journey of the Reader and the Other Reader like a shadow—that of the self-conscious. This is the 'outside' that follows the migration of/from 'inside' though one story to another. In the ambiguity of this spatial dislocation, the Reader is staying cautious against any misconception of the familiar, knowing full well how the line between the home and the world, an inside and an outside, and between the product and the process can easily blur:

> There's a boundary line: on one side are those who make books, on the other those who read them. I want to remain one of those who read them, so I take care always to remain on my side of the line.... This boundary line is tentative, it tends to get erased: the world of those who deal with books professionally is more and more crowded and tends to become one with the world of readers.... I know that if I cross that boundary, even as an exception, by chance, I risk being mixed up in this advancing tide; that's why I refuse to set foot inside a publishing house, even for a few minutes. (Calvino 93)

The 'home' here must, then, be understood both as a metaphysical as well as a material category. Tracing the genesis of a book, one takes into account all the scriptural details, the possible influences, and all the documents that have helped give the book the shape it has eventually attained. Now it is understandable that this essay does not try to address the genesis of this particular Calvino's book but rather the story titled "If on a Winter's Night a Traveller", left unfinished in favour of a narrative, should the prefatory chapters be understood thus, involving the details of a printing-binding industry that a book is a product of. The story builds up with a genetic enquiry.

Whether it is in the confinement of the palpable book or in the vents of fiction that allows imagination to travel beyond all those limitations, Calvino moves effortlessly from one book to the other, as he steers his Reader across boundaries. In an interview, Calvino was asked why he chose "such an obscure nationality" like Cimmerian for his novel which at first seemed to be Polish, after the printing-binding problem was revealed by the shopkeeper. Calvino appears rather sceptical of the critical stances and references that shape the topography of the narratives. As the narrative moved from one genre to the other, the origin equally suffered multiple shifts. Formal and generic experiments obscure the genesis only to offer a number of possible influences and borrowings. But what else help shape the narrative to denote the movement of the book that the Reader is looking for but these transnational influences disregarding national and generic boundaries? The author himself talks in terms of sensibilities and stylistic manoeuvrings instead of giving away direct genetic clues:

> Because I did not want to have precise nationalities at all. In fact, many of the critics tried to suggest precise references, claiming that one of the inserted novels would have been by this author and another novel would have been by that author. No, they are examples of styles, general suggestions rather than specific authors or literatures. The beginning of the book titled "Leaning from the Steep Slope" could be German, in terms of landscape at any rate—I recall the sea near Lübeck—but

> in terms of sensibility, it's nearer to the states of mind found in Austrian literature. (Lucente 248-49)

The cultural debates that took place in post-war Italy would provide us with the intellectual horizon within which Calvino's works need to be situated. From neo-realism to the fantasies, that Calvino has travelled in his literary career somehow validates the playful as a political category. In one of his interview, he clearly states:

> I wrote neorealist fiction because during the war I had experienced the everyday life of the people first hand. But my literary formation, insofar as one can speak of literary formation in regard to the years of my adolescence before the war, was tied very closely to Italian literature as such and did not, therefore, have very profound roots in realism. Italian literature between the two wars cannot be said to have been particularly realistic, and therefore it was not as though the realist roots went very deep. (Lucente 246-47)

While some postmodernist fictions provoke ontological reflections by projecting a plurality of worlds, others do so by troubling the very process by which the fictional worlds are constructed. Inset micro-worlds are narratologically dependent upon, and consequently ontologically weaker than, the framing worlds in which they are inset. As Henri Lefebvre would opine, "any search for space in literary texts will find it everywhere and in every guise: enclosed, described, projected, dreamt of, speculated about" (Lefebvre 15). The philosophical novelist that he has always been sees him indulge into depicting the worlds as spiral galaxies, the byways of exotic mazes, architectonics of invisible cities:

> Art begins not with flesh but with the house. That is why architecture is the first of the arts.... But however extendable this system may be, it still needs a vast plane of composition that carries out a kind of de-framing following lines of flight that pass through the territory only in order to open it onto the universe. (Deleuze 186)

The Reader journeys through unknown territories, unfamiliar domains, in search of the origin(al), the ur-text; but all the movements occur within the architectural dimension that the book assumes. The movement *from* is actually a movement *towards*. The Reader has almost no agency and still functions as a pawn in the narrative game the Calvino indulges in. The search for the story and the migration of the story across boundaries remain within a narrative that houses this search for the homely. The journey therefore is labyrinthine yet teleological, dimensional yet directional. And in these narrative detours lies the formation of the tension between the homely and the unhomely, the playful and the political, the expected and the experiential.

Works Cited

Bellemin-Noel, Jean, "Psychoanalysis and the Avant-texte" (1982) in Jed Deppman, Daniel Ferrer, and Michael Groden, eds. *Genetic Criticism: Texts and Avant-textes*. Philadelphia: University of Pennsylvania Press, 2004. Print.

Calvino, Italo. *If on a Winter's Night a Traveller*. Trans. William Weaver. London: Vintage, 2007. Print.

Deleuze, Gilles, and Félix Guattari. *What is Philosophy?* Trans. Graham Burchell. New York: Columbia University Press, 1994. Print.

Freud, Sigmund. *Writings on Art and Literature*. Foreword. Neil Hertz. Stanford: Stanford University Press, 1997. Print.

Kermode, Frank. *The Sense of an Ending: Studies in the Theory of Fiction*. New York: Oxford University Press, 2000. Print.

Kristeva, Julia. *Strangers to Ourselves*. Trans. Leon S. Roudiez. New York: Columbia University Press, 1991. Print.

Lefebvre, Henri. *The Production of Space*. Oxford: Blackwell, 1991. Print.

Lucente, Gregory L. and Italo Calvino. "An Interview with Italo Calvino" in *Contemporary Literature*, Vol. 26, No. 3 (Autumn, 1985), 245-53. Madison: University of Wisconsin Press. Web.

Malpas, Jeff. *Heidegger and the Thinking of Place: Explorations in the Topology of Being*. Massachusetts: MIT Press, 2012. Print.

17

Shifting Locations—Cordelia from *King Lear* to *Lear*

Siddhartha Biswas

In the history of stories we have seen many migrations. There are texts which have travelled, there are characters who have had journeys as remarkable as their tales. From classical times to the very modern we have seen figures like Orestes and Electra transform into different avatars and transfer to different media. They have been adapted, adopted by authorial figures as varied as Eugene O'Neil and Jean Paul Sartre. But in these cases often the inherent theme remained the same with only their identities and locations altered. But there are characters who had had to migrate completely into different arenas, not only in terms of their essential identities, but also in those of their socio-political locations.

These migrations present an interesting look not only into the imagined status of the present scene, but also into the reading of the past by the contemporary time. But there is another possible reading of this reinvention. One might say that it is difficult to negotiate with the socio-political location of actual migrants, but in the realm of imagination it is quite possible to give them lives that the present establishment might consider appropriate or suitable. Since alien cultures are often defined in terms of past *stories*, with the present remaining mostly unfamiliar, the actual migrant often presents a problem. Orientalism is one issue, but there is a parallel 'Occidentalism' that functions as well. All cultures have preconceived notions about others, and that results in exoticism or xenophobia or undue appreciation. And this model works similarly with the past. The past is either idealized or seen as barbaric. People from the past are seen either as exemplary or as villains. And their re-location in the present has always been a matter of great fascination, something that has been manipulated by commercial, theoretical or political agenda. Such figures show the passage of time and space, and their textual or extra-textual journeys become significant in understanding the dynamics behind such migration. By positing such figures in times that they do not belong, by reconfiguring their identities, the authorial voice presents the literary/political identity prevailing. These figures do not become representative of the migrants, but of the configuration that deals with them. They are not given a home, but are shown as fighting to create one. Their success or failure becomes of crucial importance in order to understand the intention of the establishment involved. Cordelia ranks quite high among these figures.

Shakespeare's Cordelia is often seen as the *ideal* woman. She is perhaps the epitome of feminine virtue—dutiful, pathologically honest, un-ambitious and beautiful. In fact, it may not be unjust to call her the perfectly crafted, 'model' character. She is exactly what society wants a daughter, a wife, even a queen to be. In her undiplomatic answer is the celebration of her innocence. But this innocence seems problematic as she, in her role as a princess, is supposed to be well-versed in diplomacy. She is supposed to be a part of the political system, and had she given a proper response to the now legendary query, it is quite a question whether she would have become a good ruler. Sigmund Freud calls her Death ("The Theme of the Three Caskets") and perhaps if she was diplomatic, she could have had a third of the kingdom and could have taken care of her father allowing a very different end to the tale. To be perfectly fair, Cordelia as well as the other sisters, find themselves inhabiting an ahistorical space, without any background or any key to what motivates them. We see them in the courtroom for the first time and we have to decipher and decode them from then on.

However, if Cordelia's responses as a daughter meet the mythopoetic demand, so does her apparently empowered action of attacking her own country, with her husband's altruistic help, to rescue it and to rescue her father. Her husband, the King of France, seems selfless and almost unconscious of the fact that if Cordelia becomes queen of Britain, he will become the King.

He may remind the audience of the kind Edward the Confessor, who helps Malcolm with his army so that justice may be served, without even the slightest inkling that Scottish history would be forever changed thereafter. Shakespeare not only earns points for showing the English need to distribute justice and civilized virtues to the corrupted and unenlightened. Cordelia's husband may not be English, but apparently Cordelia's need to help her country by defeating her sisters, along with their husbands, and giving the country to the old irrational man—irrationality that actually created the whole mess anyway—and taking care of King and country together, is what drives her husband to adopt this great virtue. She is the ultimate Princess and the exemplary Queen—not only does she intend to liberate her country, but also give her husband the opportunity to serve the very land by ruling it.

Whereas even though she mounts an attack on her own country and countrymen Cordelia has justice on her side, her sisters are not so fortunate. They are burdened with conniving natures, with greed, and the unbecoming hankering for inheritance and property. They are willing to speak untruths that shock the audience. This becomes even more apparent because Cordelia the Pure provides such a contrast. Unfortunately the ideals of purity and innocence are not there in Goneril and Regan. Not only are they proficient in flattery, they also object so unjustly to Lear's knights wrecking innocuous havoc in their households. They become villains by becoming centres of power that Lear himself has rewarded them with—and can no longer, in all practical fairness, expect to control. What Shakespeare cannot allow the audience to realize is that Lear's problem is Lear himself. By abdicating power he does not remain King anymore, but the old man never can relinquish the title or the association. And when Cordelia finally attacks to re-establish Lear, it becomes a war of aggression, because Lear's right of being a king is something he had willingly surrendered. Shakespeare, with ideals of divine right and divine loyalty, calls his play *King Lear*, never really allowing the man to fall out of royalty, thereby validating Cordelia's actions at the end.

Shakespeare relocated Cordelia as per his needs. He was largely faithful to Holinshed and other sources, but he never allows Cordelia to become the legendary queen of the pre-Roman Britain as we find in Geoffrey of Monmouth's *Historia Regum Britanniae*. Since there is no concrete historical mooring, Shakespeare could deal with the character according to his needs and he needed a tragedy showing the evil effects of division of a nation and civil war. His play focused on the romantic tragic resolution in which Cordelia must die, leaving the land in utter disarray. The establishment of the geo-political map within the popular imagination required this so-called sacrifice. This was also an artistic necessity as this allowed Shakespeare's own poetic goal to be fulfilled. As Jenny S. Spencer comments:

> Shakespeare creates a symbolic world that involves a constant shift in our perceptions away from a material reality to a spiritual one, from the concrete to the cosmic, from a particular landscape to a universal one. (Spencer 85)

Shakespeare was simply catering to the need of his age, the need of his audience and the demands of contemporary socio-political ethos.

If we stop for a moment and analyze the name Cordelia we will find it possibly comes from the Welsh name Creiddylad which means "Heart of the Sea" but Cordelia might also derive from the French *Couer de lion* or "Heart of the Lion". If we stretch the significance of the latter to suit our needs, we may find Cordelia signifying *Couer de Lear* or "Heart of Lear". There is no doubt that Cordelia remains at the focal point of all Lear stories and in her development we find the resolution to the tale.

Edward Bond, in his *Lear*, relocates Cordelia completely. In his play Cordelia is no longer a part of the royal structure. In fact, she becomes Cordelia only after a major trauma that leaves her homeless and alone. Significantly, Bond keeps only two names from the Shakespearean original—Lear and Cordelia. Whereas the first remains at the centre—sans the title King—the latter is allowed to be born. Bond's Lear story develops shakily on the lines of the Shakespearean plot which differs significantly as far as the essence of the theme is concerned. As Bond said,

> One also has to recognize that, although the Greeks created the first western democracy, it was a democracy founded on slavery. But while acknowledging the power of the Greek dramatists, what we have to do is find a way of integrating the individual dilemma with the social problem. Even Shakespeare, for all his greatness, can't always do that. (*The Guardian* Interview with Michael Billington)

At the beginning we see no third daughter. And instead of Goneril and Regan we have the daughters Bodice and Fontanelle who depose Lear through a violent coup. The issue is the building of a wall to ward off imaginary enemies. The building of this wall, as we see at the beginning, is depleting the nation's resources; and the daughters rightly protest against the irrationality and the injustice involved. The dethroned and almost insane Lear is seen roaming through the countryside and finds shelter at a farmer's household despite the objections of the Wife. By this time, the daughters not only have kept the wall intact, but are continuing its construction. Through the actions of a band of soldiers—who engage in unnecessary destruction—we see the Wife violated and widowed and finally rescued by the mysterious and symbolic Carpenter. It is at this moment that we hear her name for the first time. Even the printed version of the text shows her as 'Wife' and reveal her name only after she has been called by the Carpenter. Cordelia, therefore, seems to be born of the violence that had been engendered by Lear. So she, instead of being Lear's biological daughter, becomes his political daughter.

Cordelia goes on to be the leader, at least the figurehead of the revolution. We see her reign is as violent and as chaotic as the earlier regimes, and the construction of the Wall remains as the major policy. She becomes the dictator who must do anything to protect her administration and her policies, her people, all conform to the ethos of violence that Bond so graphically portrays. This is not the faithful daughter that earlier tellers had presented, but a 'daughter' quite true to the legacy of the 'father'.

Bond's relocation of Cordelia responds to the postmodern political atmosphere. We no longer inhabit a world of any ruling system that looks at the welfare of the people—but looks first to maintain power and will do anything to remain as the establishment. Cordelia's migration from royalty to the bottom of the social eco-system signifies a grand shift in the so-called 'grand narrative'. We no longer look for answers from above, but from the populace. Significantly, Bond does not promote any political system even though his socialistic bent is clearly expressed in every way. Power corrupts—this is the simple formula that he represents. No system will work as long as power is the central concern. And as Bond had mentioned, society must keep on changing the system and the people involved until the perfect solution—even if temporary—presents itself.

Cordelia can no longer be at home in the source of power. As the symbol of hope she must arise from the masses; even though her home is never truly established. Her new location is the farm, a home she jealously guarded, unlike Shakespeare's Cordelia, who never realized that she can be un-located with such ease. We see her as the Wife objecting to her husband, the Gravedigger's Boy, giving shelter to a man unknown and obviously deranged. She is protective and aware of the political atmosphere; she knows that the establishment can persecute anyone under any pretext. Unaware of Lear's identity, the Gravedigger's Boy gives him a home and as a result the Boy has to lose everything. Bodice and Fontanelle's soldiers are seen hunting Lear and they take the old man, 'punishing' arbitrarily the harbourers of the fugitive. The Wife loses her husband, is raped and loses her pregnancy. The violation of her self and her identity is complete. The fact that she is no more than collateral damage makes her predicament even more traumatic. Through this destruction she can be reinvented as Cordelia. She learns the hard way what it is to be dispossessed. She is no longer the returning princess fighting for justice and her right, but a figure rising out of the lower stratum who demands justice from the structure. Quite the opposite of Lear, she does not take her fate lying down and disintegrate into victimhood, but enters the world of positive action.

Bond's Cordelia does not need an invading army to disrupt the system. She finds herself at the helm of a revolution—even though we do not see how she is propelled to that position. The focus remains on Lear, and her progression is unnecessary for the text. The fact that she, the victim, soon becomes the victimizer is of greater importance. She is leading and becomes a leader. In this she becomes the earliest Cordelia, the queen. Of course, Bond does not follow Monmouth or the legends, and we do not see how Cordelia herself will end. But the creeping suspicion is that she too will find a violent end. We may take a quick look at Monmouth:

> After a peaceful possession of the government for five years, Cordeilla began to meet with disturbances from the two sons of her sisters, being both young men of great spirit, whereof one, named Margan, was born to Maglaunus, and the other, named Cunedagius, to Henuinus. These, after the death of their fathers, succeeded them in their dukedoms, were incensed to see Britain subject to a woman, and raised forces in order to raise a rebellion against the queen; nor would they desist from hostilities, till, after a general waste of her countries, and several battles fought, they at last took her and put her in prison, where for grief at the loss of her kingdom she killed herself. (*History of the Kings of Britain* 33)

Perhaps this is the most significant departure from Shakespeare—the fact that Cordelia is not allowed to die. In this location her death would probably have given her the status of a martyr, but Bond keeps the focus on Lear and it is Lear's death that is of primary significance, not Cordelia's. Her place as the revolutionary makes her the opposite of a Queen as far as the trappings of 'royalty' are concerned. The aura of authority that we find in her surpasses that we saw in Lear or in the sisters when they were the rulers. She has a political rationale. This rationale might be faulty, but she does not have the sense of arbitrariness that was the hallmark of two earlier regimes. However, that division is blurred by the hunger for power that her regime shows. Being the daughter of violence, she is free of any association with either the traditional ideas of innocence or of virtue. She is either moulded and manipulated by the revolution or she is indeed its proper leader—either way she and the power borne of the revolution become synonymous. She is the new establishment in this play.

Cordelia continues the legacy of violence that she had inherited from her predecessors. Bond is clear about violence and states quite clearly that the world cannot exist without or be shaped by anything but violence. The irony is that the violence remains the same, as does the reason behind it. Cordelia has been called a Stalin figure. In fact, Bond himself called her a "rural female Castro" (Billingham 41). But she probably represents any dictatorial system that does not take into account the people or their actual welfare. As with all the earlier rulers, Bond does not allow us to feel sympathy for Cordelia as she soon steps into the role of the oppressor. Her revolutionary status transforms into something monstrous and breaks the romantic myth of the revolutionary becoming the idea ruler. She is warned by Lear:

> Listen, Cordelia. You have two enemies, lies *and* the truth. You sacrifice truth to destroy lies, and you sacrifice life to destroy death. It isn't sane. (*Lear* 84)

Unfortunately, her migration to authority works for her and she finds 'home' in centre of power. She becomes hardened by the *realpolitik* and the realization that power can be easily removed makes her equally cruel. Instead of demolishing the Wall, she now has a need for it as her neighbouring structures would all be enemies of the revolution. So, the Wall-death they were running away from finds no remission—in fact, it remains firmly instated.

Bond's *Lear* is all about political resolution. Cordelia is not quite the fundamental message Bond wants to present and therefore she is never allowed the central position in the plot. It remains about Lear, but a Lear who is now inextricably bound with the concept of new Cordelia. In the final scene of the play we see Lear being shot by an ordinary soldier who kills the old blind man not because it was necessary, but simply because he could. In his death Lear does not achieve martyr status within the reality of the dramatic narrative, but his death makes the audience think. The fact that Lear feels compelled to act shows his evolution—he is now a true citizen who is forced into action, even though he knows that his actions by themselves will be futile. This is designed to disturb the audience and instead of giving them an emotional catharsis, makes them think about the violence and the futility of the final action. And this action is further made significant by the complete absence of Cordelia the ruler in the final scenes. She almost becomes pure power and a symbol of the problems of power-hungry structures. The play comes almost full circle in the final scene. Here, even though she is absent, Cordelia becomes a reflection of Lear as he was in the first scene. She is not the killing hand, but is directly responsible for Lear's murder. Through the young soldier we see the same cruelty, the same casual neglect of human rights and the same devotion to the Wall which had characterized Lear in the beginning. And it may not be wrong to say that the circle begins once more.

King Lear, in fact the legend of King Lear, was about the process of formation of society. *Lear* is also about society in flux. Bond shows that the structures that constitute society need constant re-visioning, they need continuous reinvention. Bond writes in his 'Author's Preface':

> Once the social structure exists it tends to be perpetuated. The organizing groups, the leaders, receive privileges. Some of these were perhaps necessary in the critical situations that created the need for leadership. But the justification for them becomes less when they are inherited by their children. At the same time they become more extensive and entrenched. They become an injustice. But the organizing group becomes self-justifying, because although its position is unjust it is the administrator of justice. (*Lear* lix)

Both the figures of Lear and Cordelia are forced to migrate into a text which contemporaries the political framework and presents the individual's altered role in the evolved arena of society. Lear is no longer King Lear and his journey now is not merely from delusion to recognition, but he must translate his realization into positive action. Cordelia must reinvent herself to locate herself into the game of power, she cannot remain the homeless and powerless princess that Shakespeare was presenting. She must also change. She must also become powerful, even if that power necessarily turns her into something vicious. It is only to be hoped that like Lear in *Lear*, she too will obtain political resolution and political recognition which will create either a new regime or a new revolution.

Cordelia's journey is not unique. She shares such migration with a number of literary characters. These characters, whether they were in search of a new home or not, are displaced from their own locations, they are stripped of their earlier identities and forced to inhabit a structure that demand complete reinvention. The demand for adaptation (or transcreation or adoption) creates this geo-temporal migration which often reflects the condition of actual migrants. Cordelia's reinvention is not a simple point of adaptation, it is an assertion of the redefinition of political identities. Her migration is an example of the trauma that migrants often have to face. The earlier Cordelia did not exactly have a happy life, from certain points of view this Cordelia fares better. But the question lies elsewhere—which life would Cordelia choose? As in case of all migration, the concept of choice becomes complicated. Since such redefinition often occurs through masculine (read patriarchal) agencies, the migrants themselves are forced to find new self-definitions whether they are willing or not. This issue of forcing people to find new identity/definition stands true of most global or personal migration. The latter happens when a person is forced into changing his own ideals and become someone else, either to preserve his/her home or to run away from intolerable circumstances. Men and women of today are pushed into migrating to different identities. The agencies that force them may be ideological, they may be political or economic, they are often religious—but in all cases it is the individual who suffers at the hands of the structure. What is lost is the question of individual choice. What can be done with impunity while dealing with literary figures cannot be accepted when such relocationing is done in the case of actual human beings. We see such dislocation—at times when the individual(s) do not even realize that they are coerced by the deep-structure—all around us. Edward Bond forcing Cordelia to become a violent dictator is a matter of literary as well as political choice. But such choices need to be examined closely and the reader/audience needs to understand how such authorities can manipulate individuals—even in the realm of reality—at will.

Works Cited

Billingham, Peter. *Edward Bond: A Critical Study*. New York: Palgrave Macmillan, 2014. Print.

Billington, Michael. "If you're going to despair, stop writing." *The Guardian*, London: The Guardian News and Media Limited, 3 Jan. 2008, www.theguardian.com/stage/2008/jan/03/theatre. Web.

Bond, Edward. *Lear*. Edited by Patricia Hern, London: Methuen Drama, 2006. Print.

Freud, Sigmund. "The Theme of the Three Caskets." *The Standard Edition of the Complete Psychological Works of Sigmund Freud*, XII, London: The Hogarth Press, 1958. Print.

Monmouth, Geoffrey of. *History of the Kings of Britain*. Translated by Aaron Thompson, Ontario: In Parentheses Publications, 1999, www.yorku.ca/inpar/geoffrey_thompson.pdf. Web.

Shakespeare, William. *King Lear*. Edited by Kenneth Muir, London: Methuen and Co. Ltd., 1965. Print.

Spencer, Jenny S. "Rewriting Classics." *Dramatic Strategies in the Plays of Edward Bond*, Cambridge: Cambridge University Press, 1992. Print.